HEIMITO VON DODERER

By MICHAEL BACHEM
Temple University

TWAYNE PUBLISHERS
A DIVISION OF G. K. HALL & CO., BOSTON

Copyright © 1981 by G. K. Hall & Co.

Published in 1981 by Twayne Publishers,
A Division of G. K. Hall & Co.
All Rights Reserved

Printed on permanent/durable acid free paper and bound
in the United States of America

First Printing

Library of Congress Cataloging in Publication Data

Bachem, Michael.
Heimito von Doderer.

(Twayne's world authors series ; TWAS 595 : Germany)
Bibliography: p. 152 - 59
Includes index.
1. Doderer, Heimoto von, 1896 - 1966—Criticism and
interpretation.
PT2607.03Z57   833'.912   80-20848
ISBN 0-8057-6437-2

TWAYNE'S WORLD AUTHORS SERIES
A Survey of the World's Literature

GERMANY

Ulrich Weisstein, Indiana University
EDITOR

Heimito von Doderer

TWAS 595

Photograph courtesy of Maria von Doderer

Heimito von Doderer

". . .Es gilt *nichts* sein zu wollen, eine Linse so klar, dass sie nur sammelt, nichts färbt."

From *Commentarii* X, September 7, 1955

Contents

About the Author
Preface
Chronology
Abbreviations
1. Beginnings and Resolve 17
2. Turning Point 49
3. The Breakthrough 68
4. Apogee 80
5. Excursion into the Grotesque 111
6. The Late Phase: *facta loquuntur* 121
7. Conclusion 142
   Notes and References 145
   Selected Bibliography 152
   Index 160

About the Author

Michael Bachem was born in Germany and came to the United States after the *Abitur*. He received his Ph.D. in German and Comparative Literature from The Pennsylvania State University. He has taught at Penn State and is now teaching German language and literature at Temple University in Philadelphia.

Preface

Judgments on the work of Heimito von Doderer vary widely. Scholars of German literature tend to rank his work alongside that of Thomas Mann,[1] or, looking particularly at the Austrian literary scene, add him to the triad of Musil, Kafka, and Broch.[2] Occasionally his novels provoke strong negative reactions. George Steiner, writing in the *Reporter*, dismisses one of Doderer's main works, *Die Dämonen* (The Demons), as "fantastically parochial," accuses the narrator of speaking with a "crotchety, gossipy voice," and calls Doderer's Vienna "a parochial town with a somewhat pompous and unsavory past."[3] On the other hand, Heinz Politzer refers to Doderer's long novels in this way: "Here, at long last, is a narrator of epics in the time-hallowed sense of the old teller of tales."[4] The verdicts of the literary marketplace will continue to vary.

This controversy applies to Doderer, perhaps more than to many other novelists, because of his determined stance as an outsider, his unwillingness to compete with the literary trends of the day, his monkish dedication to the craft of fiction. He rejected the major trends of German (as distinct from Austrian) novel writing, preferred the esoteric use of literary terminology, and separated philosophizing from novel writing (in contrast to Thomas Mann, for example). Assessing the work may become difficult because of the controversial politics of Doderer, who survived the Second World War in the uniform of a German Air Force Officer. However, one of the deeper reasons for Doderer's status as a conservative outsider is what might be called—somewhat simplistically—his embrace of the world *as it is*. He refused to pass judgment—except on *Hausmeister* or *concièrges*—and his almost instinctive, but thoroughly reasoned rejection of any and all ideologies, tend to separate and alienate him from the main literary trends and figures of postwar German literature.

Weighty arguments have been offered as to why Doderer should be counted as one of the foremost European novelists of the twentieth century. One of the leading Doderer scholars in the United States, Ivar Ivask, has enumerated seven reasons for holding Doderer in high regard; and among these, two are central to understanding Doderer's work: (1) Doderer is "one of the truly convincing realists in the German novel," and (2) "Doderer is one of the few genuine humorists among German novelists."[5] Perhaps it is ironic that due to his untimely appearance on the literary scene—everyone knows that realists and humorists belong in the nineteenth century—Doderer has suffered considerable misunderstanding.

In approaching Doderer's work, one is struck by what might be called its self-sufficiency. To be sure, Doderer was a learned man, a historian and a scholar of undoubted competence. Nevertheless, with little Latin and less Greek, his writing is easily accessible to the educated reader. If one enters the world of his writing, one soon becomes familiar with the predominant locale, Vienna, and soon knows the recurring characters, motifs, turns of phrase, in fact the "crotchety, gossipy voice" of the narrator. And—to use a Doderer device—if one remembers that the word "narrator" derives from the Latin *narrare*, that is, to tell, relate, narrate, recount, and to speak, one can easily respond to Doderer's narrative attitude. He does indeed speak to the reader, occasionally pulling his leg, cajoling him, boasting, or berating his own inadequacy. In short, his presence is rarely disguised, the reader is taken in, and quite frequently Doderer will use the embracing "we" as a narrative viewpoint. That the constant presence of a narrator is not without problems and pitfalls will be seen in the discussion of *Die Dämonen*.

The search for truth and honesty, the fierce dedication to the craft of writing, the sense of moral responsibility, the keenness of his insights, the delicate sensibility, the exuberance of his vitality—however disturbing it might occasionally seem—and the manner in which these are reflected in his writing, all this makes a study of Doderer's work a rewarding experience.

This study will trace the development of Doderer's writing from the beginnings in the early 1920s to the breakthrough in the 1930s, and to the success of the 1950s and 1960s. Orderly sequence is made difficult by Doderer's tendency to cross-reference his own works, his jumping back and forth in time, and his fundamental belief in telling stories from the retrospect of many years. This aspect, and thus the reliance on memory, is crucial to his theory of the novel. Doderer has left extensive diaries, only partially published, and a volume of critical and philosophical essays. These will be referred to inasmuch as they help to understand his fiction.

In the attempt to understand the fictional world of a writer in a language other than English one may expect difficulties because his works have not been translated or have been inadequately

Preface

translated. In the case of Doderer, the translators have been excellent ones, but, with the exception of three novels and a few short stories, his work remains untranslated. The particular difficulty with Doderer's language manifests itself in his tendency to pay extremely close attention to the exact meaning of words, and to their semantic derivation. We may encounter twice-refracted puns, esoteric usages, or plays with words that are often meaningful, yet cannot possibly be rendered into English. Consider, for example, Rittmeister von Eulenfeld, a figure in *Die Strudlhofstiege* (The Strudlhof Steps) and *Die Dämonen*. The term "Rittmeister" simply designates a captain in the cavalry, but Doderer jokingly refers to him as "Zerrüttmeister." The word derives from the verb "zerrütten," to disarrange, unsettle, disintegrate. In this way he characterizes the corrosive influence the old drunkard of a baron has on a group of young people, and the tendency of this member of the "Old School" to analyze people with his acerbic and devastating wit. Unfortunately, only a jungle of footnotes could help to indicate the complexity of Doderer's allusions. Yet Doderer himself believed in the translatability of the novel. In the following study, existing translations will be used wherever possible.

My thanks to all Doderer scholars and friends, particularly to Dr. Wendelin Schmidt-Dengler for his patient help while I was working at the Doderer archive in Vienna, to Temple University for a grant-in-aid enabling me to travel to Vienna, to K. E. Smith, my wife, for correcting my outlandish style, syntax, leaps and lacunae, and most of all to Frau Maria von Doderer for her generous help and for an unforgettable afternoon at the "Blauensteiner" and a walk through the vineyards of Grinzing.

MICHAEL BACHEM

Temple University

Chronology

1896	Heimito von Doderer born September 5 in Weidlingau (Hadersdorf), near Vienna.
1914	Graduated from the Landstrasser Gymnasium in Vienna.
1915 - 1916	Military training and service in the "k.u.k. Dragoner Regiment No. 3." Captured by the Russians after the battle of Olesza.
1916 - 1920	In various POW camps in Siberia.
1920	Escapes from Siberia, crossing the Kirghiz Steppe on foot.
1920 - 1927	Studies history and psychology at the University of Vienna.
1923	*Gassen und Landschaft* (Alleys and Landscape), poems.
1927 - 1931	Writes historical-cultural essays for several newspapers.
1930	*Das Geheimnis des Reichs* (The Mytsery of the Kingdom). Marries Gusti Hasterlik (divorced 1934). "Der Fall Gütersloh" (The Gütersloh Case).
1931 - 1936	Writes the first part of *Die Dämonen*. Joins the illegal National Socialist party in Vienna, becomes disenchanted in 1936, and was no longer carried as a party member after the *Anschluss*.
1938	*Ein Mord den jeder begeht* (English tr. *Every Man a Murderer*, 1964).
1938 - 1939	Converts to Catholicism.
1940	*Ein Umweg* (A Detour).
1940 - 1945	Participation in World War II as lieutenant, then captain in the German Air Force.
1945	Captured by the British in Norway.
1946	Returns to Vienna.
1946 - 1950	Works on *Die Strudlhofstiege;* studies at the "Institut für Österreichische Geschichtsforschung."
1951	*Die erleuchteten Fenster oder die Menschwerdung des Amtsrates Julius Zihal* (The Illuminated Windows or the

	Humanization of Councillor Julius Zihal), written in 1938 - 39. *Die Strudlhofstiege* (The Strudlhof Steps).
1952	Married to Maria Emma Thoma.
1953	*Das letzte Abenteuer* (The Last Adventure).
1956	*Die Dämonen* (English tr. *The Demons*, 1961).
1957	*Ein Weg im Dunklen* (A Path in the Dark).
1958	*Die Posaunen von Jericho* (The Trumpets of Jericho).
1959	*Die Peinigung der Lederbeutelchen* (The Torment of the Leather Pouches).
1962	*Die Merowinger oder Die totale Familie* (The Merovingians or The Total Family).
1963	*Roman No 7, Erster Teil: Die Wasserfälle von Slunj* (English tr. *The Waterfalls of Slunj*, 1966).
1964	*Tangenten, Tagebuch eines Schriftstellers* (Tangents, Diary of a Writer).
1966	*Meine neunzehn Lebensläufe und neun andere Geschichten* (My Nineteen Curricula Vitae and Nine Other Stories). *Unter schwarzen Sternen* (Under Black Stars). Dies on December 23d, in Vienna.

Abbreviations

C	*Commentarii 1951 - 1956*
DD	*Die Dämonen*
DlA	*Das letzte Abenteuer*
Erinn	*Erinnerungen an Heimito von Doderer*
E	*Erzählungen*
FP	*Frühe Prosa*
GL	*Gassen und Landschaft*
GW	*Der Grenzwald*
MER	*Die Merowinger*
Mord	*Ein Mord den jeder begeht*
M	*Every Man a Murderer*
Rep	*Repertorium*
SHS	*Die Strudlhofstiege*
T	*Tangenten*
ThD	*The Demons*
U	*Ein Umweg*
WdD	*Wiederkehr der Drachen*
WiD	*Weg im Dunklen*
WoS	*The Waterfalls of Slunj*
WvS	*Die Wasserfälle von Slunj*
Z	*Die erleuchteten Fenster oder die Menschwerdung des Amtsrates Julius Zihal*

CHAPTER 1

Beginnings and Resolve

I *The Origins*

HEIMITO von Doderer was born on September 5, 1896, in Hadersdorf near Vienna.[1] Architecture and engineering were part of the family tradition, and Doderer's paternal grandfather had been raised to nobility shortly before 1900 in recognition of his work as an architect and teacher. His father's ancestors came to Austria sometime before 1850 from Heilbronn, Germany. His mother, Luise Wilhelmine von Hügel, also came from a family of architects. Doderer's unusual first name, an affectionate form of the Spanish "Jaime,"[2] and unusual facial features—deep-set eyes, which he attributed to Mongolian influence—are among the characteristics distinguishing him from his family. He also felt that the distant relationship to the poet Nikolaus Lenau accounted for a depressive streak in his personality.

Doderer's autobiographical confessions are usually flippant and oblique. Nevertheless, when fame came to him late in life, he compiled a "Division of the Year of my Birth, 1896."[3]

Beginning of the Garden City Movement.
First Alpine ski school, in Lilienfeld, Austria.
First modern Olympic Games, in Athens.
Communal establishment of unemployment compensation:
   "Cologne Municipal Relief Fund against Unemployment in Winter."
Ludwig Rehn: first successful cardiac suture.
Discovery of the radioactivity of uranium by Bequerel (uranium
   discovered in 1786 by Martin Heinrich Klaproth).
Giacomo Puccini: *La Bohème*.
Art nouveau from Munich.
Film showings by the Lumière brothers in Paris.
R. Eucken: *The Struggle for the Spiritual Content of Life*.
H. H. Busse founds, along with L. Klages and G. Meyer, the
   "German Graphological Society."

17

Leo Tolstoy: *The Power of Darkness*
Henrik Sienkiewicz: *Quo Vadis*
Arthur Schnitzler: *The Love Game*
Rainer Maria Rilke: *Offerings to the Lares*
Gerhart Hauptmann: *The Sunken Bell*
Albert Langen and Th. Th. Heine found the political and satirical weekly *Simplicissimus* in Munich.
King Albert of Saxony guarantees the Three-Class Franchise.
Friedrich Naumann founds the "National Social Union."
Theodor Herzl: *The Jewish State* (Jewish-Zionist call for a homeland in Palestine).
Italy's war against Abyssinia.
Battle of Adua: Abyssinia defeats Italy and gains independence.

Doderer spent his childhood in District III of Vienna and in the Villa Riegelhof at Prein an der Rax. The aura of the "Wienerwald" near Hadersdorf-Weidlingau and the vicinity of the "Prater" left deep impressions on him. In many of his novels, particularly in *Die Strudlhofstiege*, he returned to the woods and meadows of his childhood. In school he was an average student, but with the help of a private tutor and extra summer courses he managed to pass the "Abitur," the final comprehensive examination, in July 1914. A schoolmate remarked later that Doderer occasionally demonstrated knowledge, which no one had expected of him.[4] In addition to Latin and Greek, a compulsory part of the school curriculum, he took private lessons in English and French. His unique ability to recall and recite long stories and poems accurately, even after a long time, does not seem to have been evident at an early age.

Doderer enrolled at the University of Vienna as a student of law, but he was called up for military service in 1915. One year later he found himself at the Russian front. In the battlefield he was promoted to ensign and then to lieutenant. During his first and only leave, Doderer began to write at his parents' villa in Prein. During this leave he also met Gusti Hasterlik, the Grete Siebenschein of his novels, with whom he was later united in a long love affair and brief marriage.

After returning to the Russian front, he took part in the battle of Olesza and on July 12, 1916, he was captured. The next four years he spent in prisoner-of-war camps in Siberia. Life in most of these camps, particularly in prerevolutionary Russia, included a considerable measure of civilization, especially for the Austrian officers. Doderer's experiences in Siberia, including the vast Russian landscape, the camaraderie, the readings, and the escape—in large

Beginnings and Resolve

part on foot—left indelible impressions. We may take a measure of how little life in the Siberian camps conforms to our preconceptions by considering that Doderer refers to the four years in Siberia as the "happiest period of his life."[5]

In his fiction Doderer returned to the Siberian experiences in one of his first novels, *Das Geheimnis des Reiches* (The Mystery of the Kingdom), as well as in his last novel fragment *Der Grenzwald* (The Forest at the Border). In Siberia Doderer read A. P. Gütersloh's novel *Die tanzende Törin* (The Dancing Fool). Gütersloh—both the work and the person—was to be of considerable influence on Doderer some years later. In prisoner-of-war camp Doderer also met Rudolf Haybach, who was to become his first publisher, after both had returned to Vienna.

In Siberia Doderer wrote the first version of the story *Das letzte Abenteuer* (The Last Adventure). He began writing a novel that later developed into one of his finest works, and also wrote most of the poems published in his first book, *Gassen und Landschaft* (Alleys and Landscape).

Just as important as personal encounters was the overall impact of the vastness of the Asian continent, witnessing suffering and degradation, the turmoil surrounding the Russian Revolution and the ensuing civil war, the adventure of the escape, and the eventual return to Vienna wearing the jacket of an English soldier. When he arrived at his parents' house, the maid at first refused to let him enter (Erinn, 17).

Three months after his return to Vienna, Doderer resumed writing his diary, which contains a continuing dialogue with himself, and provides us with an independent source book—rather than a commentary—for his fiction. On September 12, 1920, he entered the following lines:

Now, after having been in the old homeland for three months, I am resuming my notes, in the opinion that such a continuing "Journal" is necessary for me.
And now, what is most important for me to experience after these three months of violent wavering: *I'll remain with it, I'll remain with my craft*—together with my deep doubts, together with my *constantly* and *violently* occurring feeling of inadequacy—*because I cannot do otherwise!* (Journal, Heft 1)[6]

Doderer adhered to his resolve for the rest of his life. He continued writing, keeping a diary, and wavering, doubting, and examining what he believed to be his shortcomings. It is characteristic for him to renew his resolve, to repeat observations, and seemingly to begin again. Twenty-eight years later, after he had published several novels, he entered in his diary:

This past week—which went by in complete inactivity and somnolence—I decided on Thursday, August 12th, to become a writer. (T, 617)[7]

Even toward the end of his life, while writing his last novel, which was to remain a fragment, he noted, "As if I had never written a novel: that's the way I stand before this task" (GW, 244).[8]

These are not pretenses at modesty, but reflections that give a measure of the tentativeness of Doderer's self-confidence, as well as of his humility. Thus one can take at least half seriously the nineteenth of Doderer's "My Nineteen *Curricula Vitae*": "In all seriousness, my actual work consists, not of prose or verse: rather, of the recognition of my stupidity" (*ChiR*, 83).

Doderer's return to Vienna in 1920 was to a world quite different from that of 1916. The polyglot Austro-Hungarian monarchy, at least in some of its symbols a continuation of the Holy Roman Empire, had become a minor German-speaking state. A republic had been superimposed on the habits of a monarchy. Whereas Doderer's adolescence had been spent in a world that still functioned with subtle hierarchical relationships, the First World War had brought profound social changes in Europe. The 1920s were—not only for Doderer—a time of disorientation, but also of hope for the reestablishment of moral values. Major ideologies, still warring for supremacy today, began to conflict, and the search for political, social, economic, and even artistic solutions could not keep pace with new developments. Sensational journalism, fiercely attacked by Karl Kraus, a sort of H. L. Mencken of Vienna, coexisted with bewildering changes in all of the arts. For all his awareness of his surroundings, and his participation in the journalism of the day, Doderer tried, from the beginning, to separate himself, to follow no trend in literature, and to become himself. In his diary in September of 1920 he noted:

In the year 1916, shortly after my arrival in the "far east" [*sic*] . . . I was once preoccupied with the one thought: now, before anything else, you must become *yourself*. — The same is true today. You want to become an artist, a literary person, someone who works with his head, a man of the intellect, or something like that, oh that's great—you want to get to the inside.

Beginnings and Resolve

O.K. then, but completely, completely. And you better slough off all the egg shells and irresponsibilities of dilettantism from your rear! (Journal, Heft 1)

In spite or because of his own tendency toward capriciousness, Doderer began to impose a rigid discipline of work upon himself, following the dictum *nulla dies sine linea* for his entire life. Not only did he write every day, but, in the figurative sense of *linea*, imposed order upon himself. Perhaps his architect forefathers in this way asserted themselves. Also, there was a good deal of the solid middle-class citizen in Doderer, who viewed the world and the way of life of the "artist" with skepticism. His studies at the University of Vienna and his taking his doctorate in 1925 and continuing to do research in history in the 1950s attest not only to his desire to compromise with the world of his father, but seem to represent necessary exercises in self-discipline. They are tokens of bourgeois respectability.

As mentioned before, Doderer rarely reveals things or events that were important to him in his childhood, and what he does mention tends to be atmospheric rather than an enumeration of facts or data. Thus, throughout his novels, and his reflective writings, the "Prater" reappears. In *Tangenten* he observes (September 8, 1944): "Fall was here once before, about three weeks ago; it spoke to me at the 'Praterstern,' with the ripe, deep, almost decaying smell of the chestnut-lined walks, an area where even today the water of my childhood stands deepest, where it is mirrored at the bottom" (T, 237). The aura of a place—frequently evoked by smells—a stretch of river, a sudden glance into an unexpectedly open view, these tend to be as important and as haunting for Doderer as literary influences.

Doderer even denied the customary notion of influence with respect to the one writer/painter, who is most frequently cited in this regard, and whom Doderer called his "teacher" most of his adult life, Albert Paris von Gütersloh.[9] To be sure, the high moral expectations Gütersloh placed on serious literature were shared by Doderer. Certainly the reading of Gütersloh's "The Dancing Fool" or of his *Bekenntnisse eines modernen Malers* (Confessions of a Modern Painter), in the spring of 1929, affected Doderer very much, without ever leading to the imitation that is, after all, the basis of "influence."

With the same caution we might add as influences on Doderer the poetry of Rainer Maria Rilke, the psychology of Sigmund Freud, Otto Weininger, and Hermann Swoboda, the writings of Franz Grillparzer, Franz Blei, Karl Kraus, Adalbert Stifter (occasionally despised by Doderer, but occasionally referred to as Saint Adalbert), and the symphonies of Beethoven (usually referred to in the diaries as Saint Ludwig).

But Doderer did not devote, or dedicate, his life to writing because of the desire to emulate someone else. Writing was rather the only response he could find to the deepest problems of his existence. In an interview with José A. Palma Caetano, he gave a very concise answer to the question why he became a writer: "I became a writer because I felt that I could thus come to terms with life, and I wanted to come to terms with life. This is the meaning of literature for me" (Erinn, 33).

It is important to follow Doderer's development from the time of his return from Siberia to that of his first book publication in 1923. We must consult diverse journalistic ventures together with the diaries to gain some understanding of these formative years. Doderer again harks back to notes, sometimes purely mental, from his time in Siberia to help him find ways to implement a decision that he had already made. In September 1920 he entered in his diary a term he had coined in Russia, "on the lonely moment," (*vom einsamen Augenblick*) and he adds: "For a man who has made a *decision* the opinion of his contemporaries is, at least initially, of no matter. He must survive before his own forum" (Journal, Heft 1). And shortly thereafter he continues:

The consequences must be drawn. *Accordingly* you would primarily have *to learn to work* with your mind. *Your intellect*—now soft, slothful, and almost entirely unformed—*needs* at least a minimum of *acuity* to be of some use as an instrument. A mountain of knowledge and insights has to be conquered. . . . (ibid.)

Doderer never took his task lightly. He made demands upon himself that exceeded the most rigorous bourgeois requirement for hard work. One is tempted to say that he was obsessed with his task of becoming a prose writer (*Prosadichter*). Whenever he wasted time, he suffered guilt. His sexuality caused him considerable uneasiness because it seemed to interfere with the orderliness and cleanliness of his life.

In the fall of 1920 he enrolled in several courses at the University of Vienna: lectures in Austrian constitutional law, practical philosophy (social problems), state and society at the time of the Reformation and Counter-Reformation, the psychology of feelings, and a course on Rembrandt. The courses in history were particularly important to him to the extent that they would help him become a writer.

History! What a view could be gained! From the narrowmindedness of a "pseudo-view," consisting of prejudices and private affairs, compiled without insight, to penetrate to a free, purely objective, factual viewpoint. And what a pre-school for a becoming prose-writer in factual judging and clear grasp of human affairs and their development. (Journal, Heft 1)

He compiled reading lists, in the manner of an eager graduate student, and concluded that he could not speak about anything and that he had thought about nothing. Art history, the national economy, literary history, French, English, Greek, and Latin were all parts of his "study plan." Fortunately he pared down his plan, or he hardly could have found the time for creative writing.

At the same time, the notion of earning an income became important to Doderer, who did not like to rely on the generosity of his father. Encouraged by the editor Kienzl, he began writing essays for publication in Viennese newspapers. The first such publication appeared on October 16, 1920, on page three of the *Wiener Mittagszeitung* over the cryptic signature *Österreichischer Schriftsteller* (Austrian Writer). This first publication was entitled *Das russische Land* (The Russian Land) and enthusiastically described the "great Russian peasants whose heart is wide and open like the steppe. . . ."[10] A genuine love for the Russian people, and for the suffering inflicted upon them by the "Red" and "White" factions of the Russian Civil War, are manifest here and to the end of his life. It is as if he drew nourishment from the Russian experience, perhaps as Rilke did under different circumstances.

One important idea, perhaps derived from Schopenhauer,[11] emerges in this first publication, and that is the importance of physiognomy. Throughout his writing, characters are often judged from the appearance of their faces. In his first publication he observes that a landscape possesses a physiognomy similar to that of a person. Therefore, to come to grips with a description of a land presents the same problem as that posed by describing the facial features of a person, and the character that emerges through these features.

In the spring of the following year, 1921, he published another essay, this time signed, but without the *von*, which designates nobility. "From the Oldest Vienna" demonstrates his early love for the city, which was to remain the focal point of his real and fictional universe. His intimate knowledge of the history of the city would also prove invaluable in the composition of his novels. Years later, he would be able to tell precisely at what time the name of some secondary street in Vienna had been changed, and—with some flourish—would even underscore his meticulous knowledge. Here again, what may seem a trifling detail actually attests to the dedication to realism and serious craftsmanship which Doderer demanded of a prose writer.

In spite of his resolve, in spite of his conscious decision to become a novelist, writing did not come easily to Doderer. His diary attests to his struggle to overcome what he called "inertia." He confesses taking every opportunity to avoid having to write. He never quite resolved the conflict between his notions of the saintliness of hard work, and his profligate tendencies. But on a deeper level, pessimism did tend to paralyze him. He underlined in his diary of the fall of 1920: "Rather chopping wood than thinking! And then to write: what a terrible activity: to sleep after a meal or to go to a café is 10 times more beautiful" (Journal, Heft 1).

Nevertheless, with the encouragement of friends Doderer continued writing, and in 1923 his friendship with Rudolf Haybach, a fellow inmate at the Siberian prisoner-of-war camp, led to his first book publication, a volume of poems entitled *Gassen und Landschaft*. The twenty-seven poems were handwritten by Haybach, transferred to lithographic plates, and printed on Haybach's own press. The binding was done by a friend.

With some exceptions the poems lack the lyrical touch, but Doderer touches themes which will remain distinctly his. One of these, as the title suggests, is the juxtaposition and interpenetration of city and country, or of inside and outside. Already in the first poem, "Prèlude," Doderer concentrates on a characteristic situation: the poet, alone in his room, senses the "moving expanse" (*bewegte Weite*) outside. At a certain moment, for no apparent reason, the poetic imagination transcends and at the same time experiences time and place very intensely. We also find in this first published poem a metaphor which will assume greater significance in later works. Doderer speaks here of the "humming depth of the moment" (*summende Tiefe des Augenblicks*). The conjunction of the notion of time with the notion of space pervades Doderer's writing, as is most obvious from the subtitle of one of his major novels *Die Strudlhofstiege:* "Melzer or the Depth of the Years" (*Melzer oder die Tiefe der Jahre*). Frequently, as mentioned earlier, a glance into a body of water may evoke a sense of the past, a sense of time having passed, and an attempt to come to a clearer understanding of self.

Some of the imagery of Doderer's poems also shows their affinity to the literary and artistic style known as Expressionism. Again, the first poem in this collection contains the image of the "wreckage of time." Similarly stark imagery and typically Expressionistic themes can be found in the poem *Bahnhofshalle* (Train Station). The hall from which the trains leave is depicted as if it were a gigantic mouth, and the station itself is addressed with a certain grandiose pathos:

> From you the trains storm forth.
> From your mouth of glass and steel you send forward
> Him whose life once
> Fell for a while on journey and distance.[12]

But poems of this kind do not predominate. Many are melancholy in tone, some are written in the vein of Heinrich Heine, for example, "Das Rendezvous" (The Rendezvous), which begins:

> Here comes the beauty of all beauties—
> Delighted that you are on time:
> All other nonsense I'll get used to.[13]

Throughout the love poems and their various descriptions of scenes, moods, and times of day, there persists the juxtaposition of the impermanence of human affairs and relationships, and the quiet permanence of the land, the river, and nonhuman reality.

In 1957 Doderer published a second volume of poetry, *Ein Weg im Dunklen* (A Path in the Dark), which includes a few of the poems from *Gassen und Landschaft*. But with some exceptions his lyrical statements remain merely interesting footnotes on his life. They yield glimpses into his biography, occasionally distinguished by particular poignancies like those written during Doderer's years as an air force officer in the Second World War, when he was briefly stationed in France. The French Symbolists, especially Baudelaire and Valéry, had always been important and interesting to him. Doderer's reaction to the atmosphere of their country led to some reflective and frequently bitter poetry. The best is the cycle "Der Flügel" (The Wing), which takes its title from a quotation by Baudelaire, who observes in his diary that on a particular day he "felt the wind of the wing of madness pass over him" ("j'ai senti passer sur moi le vent de l'aile de l'imbecillité").

Even though Doderer had finished the manuscript of his first short novel, *Die Bresche* (The Breach), in 1921, it was not published until 1924, having been rejected by one publisher. In the years before the publication of his first major prose work, the struggles with his somewhat miserly father persisted and the war of the artist and the bourgeois within himself continued. This struggle was intensified by his relationship with Gusti Hasterlik, who reinforced the need for steady income and respectability. Their relationship seems to have been at best unpredictable, and at worst painful, for both. Nevertheless, on February 13, 1922, he wrote in his diary: "The beloved *is everything*, my second life. . ." (Journal, Heft 2).

In the meantime, he continued a far-flung, eclectic reading program, which included Stendhal's *The Red and the Black*, Spengler's *The Decline of the West*, and Freud. A diary entry from September 16, 1922, reads: "From him [Freud] I now get my 'wisdom.' " He mentions having read Oscar Wilde, particularly *The Critic as Artist, The Decline of Lying*, and *The Ideal Husband*. In 1923 he comments on having read Thoreau's *Walden:* "What a critique of life, which in the end, avoids life itself?"

He mentions attending a performance of the *Saint Matthew Passion*, is impressed by Wagner's "description" of a sunrise, and begins his veneration of Beethoven. On August 13, 1923, he writes: "I want to buy his death mask, I want to own it and always be able to look at it. He remains *the* hero to me and *the* man, and I love him from my filth [*aus Meinem Dreck heraus*], in my way, and as well as I can" (Journal, Heft 2). The tight-lipped countenance of Beethoven which Doderer has in mind, and from which we can infer so much determination, fits Doderer's own struggle and dedication to becoming a writer.

While the problem of models or influences is always a difficult one, in the case of an eccentric like Doderer it becomes particularly elusive. Nevertheless, Doderer himself mentions in his diaries, in addition to the names already enumerated, A. P. Gütersloh, Lao Tse, Stefan George, Max Dauthendey, Eduard Mörike, Baudelaire, Zola, Schopenhauer, Unamuno, Pirandello, and—in 1925—comments on Kafka's "Process" (*sic*): "One of the best of all books I know."

Doderer's diary of the early 1920s also examines the precise effect of various stylistic devices, questions the appropriateness of certain verb tenses for narrative or for descriptive prose, and considers the rhythm and length of sentences, even their "tempo." He attempts to describe by means of diagrams the structure and the tension of a sentence, and, somewhat later, of entire stories, or sections of novels. Not only do the architect ancestors assert themselves in these attempts, but the constant and lifelong attention of Doderer to the craft aspect of his work becomes evident.

Certain characteristics of his writing begin to emerge. He asks himself: "Does the genuine narrative artist have to consider his readers during the production?" And providing his own answer: "He doesn't *have to*, i.e., during the central, important acts of production he will certainly not consider him!—if he has anything of the artist in himself" (Journal, Heft 2).

In these formative years, Doderer begins to evolve a certain narrative attitude, coupled with certain narrative forms which are distinctly his own. One central aspect of these forms and attitudes is that they are directed at an audience. The "Divertimento," a literary form patterned after the loosely structured musical model, becomes highly audience oriented. In fact, Doderer intended the "Divertimenti" to be read aloud at one sitting. He himself memorized some of his "Divertimenti," and *told* them to live audiences in Vienna, without so much as a cue card. His sister attests that he did not miss a word of the written text. Doderer laboriously trained his powers of memorization, not only by learning his own works by heart, but by memorizing long sections from Schopenhauer's philosophical writings. (DW, 267).

The notion of *telling* or narrating past events, the Homeric attitude, becomes a central aspect of Doderer's major novels and, inasmuch as he succeeds, a central part of their unique charm. This attitude implies, among other things, a temporal distance, by relating events as they are developing. This does not mean that Doderer writes historical novels. One characteristic that clearly distinguishes his novels from so-called historical novels is the constant intervention of the narrator who creates various levels of time as well as keeping the awareness of temporal distance alive in the reader.

In Doderer's diary entries from the early 1920s, there persists much struggle and pain. Even a measure of self-hatred enters into Doderer's inner life. On August 4, 1926, he excerpts a quote from Unamuno: "Perhaps the hatred of one's self, of the own blood, is the only possibility to free one's self from the hatred of others" (Journal, Heft 4). But the genuine joy he experienced during the creative process balanced this hatred. Thus he writes in January 1922:

What is the most beautiful, the most magnificent state of being? The most beautiful is when your brain furiously tries to split, to penetrate, and finally to express the material which is driven up from below (still raw, in unformed blocks, in barbarian, primitive images). Compared to this state, all joys and lusts which may be conceived, are miserable cat shit. (Journal, Heft 2)[14]

Occasionally the distractions he experiences are slightly adolescent, and certainly amusing; he calls them *lausbübisch* (punky). The view from his window sometimes permits him to watch women undress themselves. For more careful observation he uses binoculars. These rather harmless episodes of voyeurism are later incorporated into one of his most delightful novels, *Die erleuchteten Fenster oder die Menschwerdung des Amtsrates Julius Zihal* (The Illuminated Windows or the Humanization of Councillor Julius Zihal).

II Die Bresche *(The Breach)*

From the retrospect of a rather brief span of time Doderer once observes about his first two published works (*Gassen und Landschaft* and *Die Bresche*) that they have the charm of youthful talent. He refers to them as remaining "round and sunny and fresh."[15] As an afterthought he mentions that *Die Bresche* was originally entitled "Divertimento," and even though this designation was later abandoned, the short novel retains the characteristic four sections or movements of Doderer's other Divertimenti. More important than the structure is the tone of the story. In the first sentence, Doderer already strikes the pose of the apologetic narrator: "In this story three main figures will appear to entertain the reader as well as they can."[16] These three are Jan Herzka, son of a well-to-do industrialist, Magdalena Güllich, Herzka's lover, and S. A. Slobedeff, known as "Fräulein Sascha," a Russian composer of uncommon insight.

Jan Herzka has grown up with a high regard for well-regulated appetites, and, his existence runs its course as if on tracks, along the "straight line of his daily life" (FP, 8). Doderer speaks of the habits and circumscriptions that guard Herzka as if they were physical barriers. In fact, the words *Umhegung* and *Gehege* are often used in German to refer to a wildlife preserve, an apt symbolic omen, because the story tells how Jan Herzka suddenly breaks through the fence of convention and proper, respected behavior, and creates a breach in the surrounding wall.

The conflict within the protagonist begins as he is casually browsing through an old bookstore to buy a present for Magdalena when suddenly he catches sight of an old illustrated volume, a so-called *Passional*, depicting the torture of female martyrs. Immediately Herzka feels driven to reenact one of the torture scenes with his gentle lover Magdalena. After the two attend a circus performance, Herzka acts out his fantasies in a shabby boarding house, and then abruptly abandons the beaten Magdalena.

The contrast between the civilized, deliberate, almost ritualistic

Beginnings and Resolve

departure of Herzka from his office in the late afternoon, and the violent, door-slamming departure from the suffering Magdalena is stark indeed. And Doderer takes pains to emphasize the contrast. At the office, Herzka is described as washing his hands, carefully checking his pockets, instructing the office boy to lock the doors carefully, whereupon he steps out into the open. Doderer then describes the feeling of liberation Herzka experiences while walking through the city in the late afternoon. It is as if he had suddenly been freed from the contemplation of numbers and were suddenly able to let his glance roam. He steps into a multitude of colors ("the last, passionate red of the evening" "violent green-gold of the gardens," FP, 10) and sees crowds of faces streaming past him, all under the "slanted sun." At the end of the first section, after the torture, "Jan took his hat, left the room, and threw the door shut with a loud crash. . . . He walked as if slightly drunk or like a sleepwalker, smooth, secure. . ." (FP, 22).

The theme of the discovery of instinctual, primitive urges is typically Expressionistic. Other aspects of the story also clearly date it as Expressionistic prose: the contrast of the safe bourgeois life on the outside which hides the equally real inner chaos, and the contrast of the restraints of traditional civilization and the presumed freedom of a new way of life.

The style, the images, and the metaphors reinforce the Expressionistic nature of the work. The hectic sentences without verbs: "The houses dark, high; all windows dead, nowhere a light" (FP, 23). Or, later during a second episode of violence Herzka sits in a tree observing a party in a house, and discovers that he is bleeding slightly from a wound in his hand, but he initially pays little attention to it. Herzka's reaction takes the form of a short monologue: "'Blood, blood. . . ,' he stammered again and again, and then, Humans [*Menschen*], humans. . . . Yes! We humans!'" (FP, 29). Apparently incoherent stammering uttered during a rush of feeling is surely typical of Expressionistic prose writing.

But more than that, through skillful use of symbols Doderer emphasizes Herzka's sense of guilt. The recurring image of a cathedral, presumably Saint Stephen in Vienna, haunts the protagonist: "Herzka stood suddenly, he looked up at the severe, old, gray face of the cathedral, whose windows looked at him with raised eyebrows. . ." (FP, 13). The paternal image of the cathedral pervades the story. Not only does it function as a reminder of a punishing godhead, which—in a dream—is walking toward Herzka but it is also linked to time, since the bells of Saint Stephen, like most German and Austrian churchbells, chime at regular intervals. For Jan Herzka time is, for a while, out of joint. He "falls out of time" (FP, 24), breaks his wristwatch, and almost automatically tosses it across the street. The persistence of external time, however, is immediately underscored: Just as Herzka hears his broken wristwatch hit the street, a churchbell chimes loudly: "A towerclock gave two rings, reverberating loudly. It seemed to him as if the iron hammer had hit the immense starred dome itself. Now the sound was trickling from its walls. . ." (FP, 23).

After the episode of sadism Herzka walks through the streets of the city, apparently without aim, stops in a dive to eat something, gets into a fight, shoots his pistol into the air to scare his pursuers, but finally escapes. Throughout this escapade Herzka is quite jubilant: "In a glow he sank into such images, rejoiced in his innermost self, as if he had reached fulfillment, a condensation of his dreams" (FP, 26).

Herzka continues his wandering to the outskirts of the city. Toward morning he finds a boat, manages to get it into the water, and as soon as he is comfortably drifting down the Danube, he falls asleep. At this point, true to the musical model, Doderer interjects an "Intermezzo," which describes the plight of Magdalena, abandoned, beaten, and in pain. Doderer again stresses the contrast between the multitude of sensations Herzka experienced when he stepped outside, and the leaden, lifeless feeling of the tortured Magdalena: "The houses, dark, high, all windows dead, nowhere a light, and the motionless air of the summer night was like a warm, dark cloth around mouth and nose. Not a single scent filled or enlivened this air" (FP, 23).

The third section or movement is taken up by Herzka's dream images. These focus upon scenes from his youth, experiences of fearful and even terrifying situations, images of destruction, as well as feelings of liberation. Herzka imagines clinging to the end of a gigantic pendulum that swings out into the dark. Again there occurs the image of the gigantic time-telling dome which rings with blows from an iron hammer. But in his dream Herzka finds liberation in the sudden discovery that he can fly. The streets of the city through which he has wandered have turned into the various directions of the points of the compass, symbolically indicating the multiple possibilities of fate.

The description of a dream on a drifting boat recapitulates the main events of the preceding evening. In the dream, however, the events are abbreviated, intensified, and sometimes slightly distorted.

Magdalena is envisioned as breaking the wall of the room that surrounds Herzka, and it is as if Herzka were subconsciously blaming Magdalena for causing him to destroy the safe and comfortable boundaries that have defined his life heretofore. In the dream, Magdalena's eyes are seen as "terrifyingly pitiless" (FP, 45).

The notion that through sadism, fighting, running away, and radical departure from everything he holds in high regard, something positive might come, is symbolically expressed in the dream, when suddenly Herzka's fall becomes flight: "Suddenly he knows how to fly" (FP, 45).

One image recurs frequently: the search for the center of a multiplicity of paths. Herzka seems to need not only a center of his life, but a new beginning, a point from which hundreds of paths lead outward. In his dream he compares his old existence to sitting in an open field with the furniture and implements of his office around him. Hundreds of people stare at him; ostracized, emaciated, bloody, and dirty, and then suddenly perched in a tree. Herzka's dream culminates in the cathedral's marching toward him in a threatening, terrifying manner, an unmistakable allusion to the walking statue in *Don Giovanni*. As the bells begin to reverberate, the drifting boat scrapes onto the sandy banks of the river and Herzka awakens somewhere in the quiet countryside.

From the hectic present tense of the third "movement" (one might call it a macabre Scherzo) the narration in the fourth section switches to the calm tones of the simple past tense. Sunlight and the now pleasant sounds of churchbells surround Herzka. The mood is pastoral. Herzka—for the first time since the preceding afternoon—considers what time it might be. "And now came the *time*—" (FP, 51). He bathes in the river, washing off the blood and sweat of the previous night's escapades, rests and even finds a chocolate bar in one of his pockets. Slowly he returns to practical considerations, but he is determined to rest and restore himself in the country. Herzka then walks along a railroad track, jumps onto a train, rides through the countryside, and as the train approaches a charming little village, jumps off, falling quite literally onto the back of a man who is sitting behind a bush and serenely puffing on a cigarette. No *deus ex machina* could be more abruptly introduced, for it is none other than the famous Russian composer S. A. Slobedeff, affectionately known as "Fräulein Sascha," who becomes Herzka's symbolic brother, guide, and prophet.

After Slobedeff has installed Herzka in a country inn, has given him a chance to rest, Herzka begins to tell him about his experiences, his inability to understand his destructive and sadistic drives, and his pervasive fear of being cast out from the orderly world he had lived in. Interestingly, a metaphor which the narrator has used early in the story to describe Herzka's sudden break of the walls of convention now enters Herzka's mind. He describes the drive that pushed him into "action" as "the. . .back of some unknown, evil, wild, abysmal monster" (FP, 68).

Slobedeff has a knack for putting ideas succinctly and he summarizes the theme of the novel. As Herzka stammers, "I no longer am. . . ," Slobedeff replies, "I believe you *were* not. And I believe that you are *not yet*. But I hope with all my heart that you *will be*. Until last night you were a boy. . ." (FP, 69). Repeatedly, Slobedeff discusses Herzka's story using the image of the breach and the breakthrough into a new life of increased insight into one's self. He stresses the importance of recognizing one's destructive drives and consequently rendering them less harmful. That raising the subconscious to the surface for inspection is nearly synonymous with "cure" is one of the central theories of psychoanalysis.[17] In this particular case, the acceptance of life, perhaps a kind of vitalism, includes a reverence even of our darker urges. Slobedeff speaks of the "reverence for the overpowering force of our blood. . .reverence for the great darkness inside and outside" (FP, 73).

Doderer's experiences in Russia, which nurture so many of his works, also emerge in this story. Slobedeff praises the Russian landscape, its expanse, its freedom—symbolized by the open steppes—and, more importantly, the "Russian soul," which for a long time seems to have realized the coexistence of conflicting urges within us, rather than resisting them as the more civilized Westerner has. Slobedeff gives an example of his own spontaneity by way of explaining his presence in this nondescript village: as he was passing through by train on his way from Luxembourg to Vienna, he suddenly felt impelled to get off at this particular village, for no apparent reason, and he followed his urge then and there.

Herzka does not know initially that his new friend is the great Russian composer whose symphony "The Adventurer" he has always admired, but he soon finds out, and thereafter the two return to Vienna together. As the train enters the city and approaches the railroad station, the fourth movement ends with a flourish of images. The luminous city "tore the night sky," "took away its curvature," and "beat the stars to death" (FP, 84). Into the deafening clanging of the train passing over switches, Slobedeff screams: "God—with—you—be brave," followed by the words: "Immediately thereafter the engine broke into a brief, triumphant howl and was gliding more and more slowly with piercing hisses under the high arch of the station hall" (FP, 84). The clanging of the switches symbolizes the multiplicity of choices that confront Herzka upon his return to the city.

At the end of the story Herzka attends a performance of Slobedeff's "The Adventurer" conducted by the maestro himself. The words sung in this symphony are included, and they seem to be curiously applicable to Herzka, because they tell about one who is not content to subordinate himself to the prevailing order, who is attempting to forge his own life, and in the end accepts the "furious breadth of life" (FP, 90). The culmination of the symphony combines a description of the open Russian landscape with the idea of a multiplicity of fates, and celebrates the person who can be a servant (*Knecht*) to both.

During the climax of this performance Herzka experiences what might be called a mystical moment: "Amid this furious roar [of the music] Herzka felt the core of his own being: and, like a piece of iron, he held it into the white fire of the Russian, and hardened his own being" (FP, 90). Doderer then quickly ends the story, saving the last and kindest words for Magdalena, describing her as a silent, kind, and great suffering spirit.

Seen within the context of Doderer's development as a writer, *Die Bresche* is important in Doderer's development not only because he creates characters who are to reappear in later works, and because it is an exuberant, youthful novel, but also because it represents the first treatment of the theme of *Menschwerdung* or "humanization" which must be considered central to Doderer. Humanization involves deep insight into oneself, acceptance of the world as it is, complete avoidance of all ideologies; and no matter how this fundamental change is accomplished, the theme is, in the final analysis, a mystical one. Because the crucial insight is often gained in a flash, sometimes brought about by arbitrary, sometimes dreamlike events; it is, at any rate, not comparable to the plodding development of the so-called *Bildungsroman*.

We can see how this theme is treated through the example of Herzka: He possesses a flaw (a tendency to sadism), which he has covered up successfully. At a certain point a chance event (browsing in the bookstore) provides enough impetus for a coming together of inner inclination and external force, and therefore for a crisis which is usually destructive. The hero may or may not survive the struggle, but if he does, he usually comes to an understanding of what happened, so that eventually he will arrive at a point where he can fuse his old existence and his new insight. Thus he begins to live in a renewed and humanized way. Frequently there is a *punctum nascendi*, such as Herzka's mystical moment at the Slobedeff symphony when the "old" and the "new" briefly touch, one integrating the other.

Doderer stresses the internal or spiritual aspects of Herzka's decisive change. As in most of his other works, the protagonist frequently experiences a moment when inside and outside are confused, when a person contemplates an external event which he suddenly sees as an interpretation or reflection of his thoughts, emotions, or even his essence. This moment of mystical intensity is experienced by Herzka during the musical performance. Doderer does not show him as a better citizen or gentleman, nor does he bother to reintegrate Herzka into society. Rather, he places a great deal of emphasis on the unquestioning acceptance of mystical events, however random or irrational they may seem. In fact he later develops a theory about the importance of seemingly peripheral events.[18] He believes that in a contemplative state the mind will focus on what are at first considered to be insignificant events, but that later developments will show that these events, images, or metaphors are of greater importance than those selected rationally. Doderer—who had read Freud with enthusiasm—seems to believe in the higher wisdom of the subconscious, and in the significance of revelations accessible to us in dreams.

Positive characters in Doderer's works often distinguish themselves by their willingness and ability to accept the validity of events at the periphery. This resultant willingness to accept a degree of irrationality, unpredictability, or randomness is expressed by one of the most frequent groups of metaphors in Doderer's work: those indicating openness—such as windows, views from unobstructed areas, open curtains, or open eyes. In one of his "Nineteen *Curricula Vitae*" Doderer expresses this idea with typical understatement: "First you break windows, then you become one."[19]

Reaching a state where one is able to let unpredictable and possibly disordered reality flow into one's consciousness, without attempting to manipulate, interfere, rearrange, or control it is seen not only being highly desirable for his protagonists, but it is also one of the fundamental prerequisites for a novelist. The struggle to accept reality without the imposition of preshaped expectations, without any ideology, was seen by Doderer as the basic struggle toward becoming a novelist. In its extreme form, his ideal is stated in the motto to this monograph: "...What is necessary is to want to become *nothing*, a lense so clear that it gathers everything and discolors nothing."[20] Imposition of ideology or of preconceived expectations on the richness and intransigence of life is seen by Doderer as a manifestation of arrogance at best, or as a prelude to murderous totalitarianism at worst.

And, finally, *Die Bresche* adumbrates another of Doderer's important philosophical themes: the conflict between "first" and "second" reality, between the world as it is and as one might wish it to be. This conflict harks back to the disputes of Medieval Scholasticism, and Doderer clearly favored the Realism of Saint Thomas Aquinas.[21] The working assumption for Doderer thus is that the world he portrays in his novels can be recognized and understood, that this world is not merely the chimera postulated by Kantian Idealism, and that it is possible to portray the world's complexity in works of fiction. In his essay "Grundlagen und Funktion des Romans" (Bases and Function of the Novel) Doderer maintains that the tendency of modern novelists such as Joyce, Proust, and Musil has been to create a "utopian or transreal novel" whereas Doderer sees as his task the conscious and purposeful "reconquering of the outer world."[22]

In *Die Bresche*, the world of Herzka before his distintegration can be described as "impoverished," a term Doderer uses to describe his idea of the second reality. Herzka's world seems like a rigid construct that leaves out or does not wish to recognize important, albeit disturbing aspects of psychological and emotional reality. His life of comfortable habits and routine gestures is threatened and partially destroyed by the interference of first reality. Acceptance of first reality and achieving humanization are linked.

These themes reemerge in Doderer's work with greater complexity and in more interesting and problematic contexts, where the phenomenon of the "second reality" is linked with notions of evil, of ideology, of political "movements," and of spiritual and intellectual myopia.

III *"Jutta Bamberger"*

"No character from his entire work preoccupied Doderer as frequently and for as long a time as did Jutta Bamberger..." (FP, 263), writes Hans Flesch-Brunningen in the notes to the volume in which the fragment "Jutta Bamberger" was first published in 1968. One reason why it remained unfinished was suggested by

Wolfgang H. Fleischer: In writing "Jutta Bamberger" Doderer found himself caught in a contradiction between wanting to create an experiment with a new form, a so-called "de-centralized" novel with several narrative centers, and the biographical or "monographic" character of the story of Jutta Bamberger. However, Doderer did not find a way to reconcile theme and structure in the experiment.[23]

Nevertheless, publication of this novel fragment has led to its being called a missing link in the development of Doderer's narrative technique.[24] The link can be seen between the strictly monographic nature of *Die Bresche* and the next published work of Doderer, *Das Geheimnis des Reiches* (The Mystery of the Kingdom), published in 1930. It is the first decentralized novel, one in which the action is not told in a single and simple time sequence, but rather breaks off, switches to another character and another action, and returns again to repeat the process.

One prerequisite for successful composition of such a novel is elaborate planning. Wendelin Schmidt-Dengler has carefully demonstrated the compositional schemes, Doderer's consideration of various narrative tenses, the construction of parallelisms, and again and again the indirect approach to the main character, Jutta Bamberger.[25] It is as if he wished to describe Jutta by showing us her reflection in others.

For all its experimental qualities, "Jutta Bamberger" still shares aspects of Expressionistic prose: the use of articles is restricted, lyrical passages enter into the work, and the big-city background is emphasized.

In modern German literature, "Jutta Bamberger" ranks among the most sensitive portraits of youth, adolescence, and troubled sexuality in conflict with its surroundings. The poetry of Rilke was Godfather, and in February 1926, after he had stopped working on "Jutta Bamberger," Doderer even noted in his diary a specific Rilke sonnet (I, 2 from the *Sonnets to Orpheus*) which begins and ends with the words "almost a girl" (*Und fast ein Mädchen wars. . . Ein Mädchen fast.*).[26]

Doderer has summarized the important facts of Jutta's life, which follow in shortened paraphrase: Jutta Bamberger, coming from an energetic-active father and a simple-female mother (*Weibchen-Mutter*), can look forward to smooth tracks of joyful-smug bourgeois well-being. But Jutta shows signs of being "different" when she is still a child. The continuing and increasing contrast to the prevailing expectations of life appear to some (sometimes to herself) as a failure

Beginnings and Resolve 37

of her femininity, particularly since this femininity forms the essential basis for such a "tracked" life (*gebahntes Leben*). . . . So that she will not be pushed aside completely, and so that she may take part in the happy life, Jutta tries hard to cast a bridge, which makes it necessary "to deny her own nature to herself." She becomes engaged, but shortly before her marriage her self-deceit becomes evident. Nevertheless, there remains the hope that the "shortcoming" is due to the lack of external stimuli, and that she is merely waiting for her real awakening. Jutta then meets Slobedeff at a masked ball, where she is disguised as a man and he as a woman. They fall in love, each mistaking the other's sexual identity. After discovery and a brief spurt of hope, despair sets in again, because Jutta cannot cope with the possessive will of Slobedeff, who is very much a "male," in spite of his feminine physique. This and other external factors, produce a conflict which "tears open Jutta's soul to the bottom of her childhood." The unbearable pressures lead, in a moment of confusion and hysteria, to suicide in her twenty-sixth year.[27]

Like Jan Herzka, Jutta grows up in bourgeois safety. The relationship of parents and children—Jutta has a brother and twin sisters—represents a model of superficiality and insensitivity. Karl and Jutta both suffer terribly, because they are intensely receptive. Doderer takes pains to describe the acute eyesight and hearing of Jutta and Karl, as well as to underscore the impressionable nature of a very young person. Even though Karl does not always understand what the adults are talking about, "for [him] a twisted mouth, a furtive glance, a soft smacking of the lips, a wrinkle in the forehead—the soul lay there ready to be inscribed and tender like a phonograph plate" (FP, 98). To the consternation of her parents, Jutta does not like to play with dolls, does not jump around squealing in her parents' bed, and has a penchant for climbing trees and peering out into the landscape.

Doderer develops the description of Jutta's eyes and the attitude of her body into a leitmotif: ". . .And the eyes (as if they led into the head, somewhat like illuminated paths, the point of origin of the glance way back there), and these eyes, very large, they were always slightly veiled, half-closed.—This is how she often stood: glancing to the side, the arms slightly pulled up, as if the hands were stopping in the middle of a motion, as if she had something to guard, or as if she were listening intently" (FP, 103). Jutta and Karl—who is so ugly that he is known as "the ape"—become outsiders, in part because both are endowed with the ability to listen (*lauschen*) and to see more and with greater intensity than the rest of their family. They also develop a special relationship to the landscape from which they take solace:

The darkness approached the house from the surrounding park; here and there a light flashed in the distance, and their own villa opened illuminated window-eyes. . . . Jutta flowed into the great quiet; as if expanded, she placed her glance into the landscape [*legte sie den Blick in die Landschaft*] . . . which entered the darkness secretively and quietly—and yet there was something magnificent, good, reassuring behind this quiet hardness. (FP, 109)

Repeatedly, Jutta and Karl find places from which to look far out over the city. Especially at the end of the first section, when Karl's departure is imminent, Jutta is twelve years old and Karl is sixteen, and the two sit on a rocky promontory from which they can overlook the city. Karl attempts to tell Jutta of his conflicts with his own sexuality, which cause him to want to leave Vienna and finish school elsewhere. He has been to houses of prostitution and feels repelled by them and by his experience there. While he cannot bring himself to tell Jutta clearly and clinically why he wants to leave, he does manage to connect the city with feelings of repulsion. Struggling for words to make his feelings clear to his twelve-year-old sister, he suddenly points to the city: ". . . She looked down into the city mass, saw the gigantic grey animal, spread far apart, bearing its long row of shining light-teeth. She understood nothing; but she felt deeply threatened" (FP, 115).

This scene again combines numerous elements of Expressionism: the struggle of a young person with inchoate sexuality; a connection of the city with evil; the juxtaposition of city (sin) and country (innocence); some striking and somewhat exaggerated metaphors (city—gigantic animal) reminiscent of the poetry of Georg Heym; and the ecstatic style of the dialogue between brother and sister, Karl kneeling before Jutta, crying, sobbing, embracing, kissing.

The next section shows Jutta attending a coeducational school and relating to a new circle of friends, among whom Schlaggenberg is closest. Schlaggenberg is initially surnamed Hans, but within a few pages his name is changed to René, a favorite with Doderer, and the name given also to his alter ego René von Stangeler. The name also suggests that of René (Rainer) Rilke, and of course—a practice never to be neglected by Doderer—it has a literal meaning derived from the Latin "renatus," born again. Thus Doderer links René to the idea of humanization (*Menschwerdung*).

Beginnings and Resolve 39

The action of the second section has its focal point in a bathing scene. A group of boys and girls, among them Schlaggenberg and Jutta, go swimming in a lake in the forest. Doderer takes the opportunity to emphasize the difference between Jutta and her "normal" girl friends. The outing of the group is vibrant with adolescent sexuality. Frogs in a pond are observed mating, which leads to a series of more or less innocent jokes, which do not bother Jutta very much. But at another instance, when Schlaggenberg playfully kisses Flora's neck, Jutta experiences almost physical pain, which is not at all jealousy. Rather, Jutta is perturbed by the atmosphere of sensuality, not by a particular instance of it. She runs off into the water and swims to the other side of the pond, her slim body as "graceful as . . . a swimming ring snake" (FP, 125). Her friends, however, interpret her flight as a simple and slightly ridiculous instance of jealousy and an attempt at punishing her friend Schlaggenberg. Actually, Jutta is amazed at her own actions and tentatively concludes that she finds the toying "unbearable."

At this point Doderer begins a formal experiment by dividing the page into two columns each of which describes a separate but simultaneous action. Although complete simultaneity, such as on a split screen, cannot be achieved, the effect is not altogether lost, because while reading in one column, the eye can stray easily to the other side to check the progress of the other action. Nevertheless, Doderer does not use this technique again. It is clear from his diaries that he took great interest in the techniques of cinematography and even attempted to transfer the techniques of film to the prose narrative. The above experiment may be seen as one such attempt.[28]

After the return of the group to the city by train, Jutta and Schlaggenberg—now renamed René—walk together, find a park and a bench. René begins an elaborate apology for his "transgression," to which Jutta listens with growing amazement, because she does not feel at all jealous or hurt. She simply functions and feels in a different but individualistic manner. At one point, when Schlaggenberg questions her about having run (or swum) off, adding that she must have been hurt by his action, she replies: "Yes . . . but not because it was you. . ." (FP, 135), an answer which René neither hears nor understands. She then asks him to kiss her, but his impetuous, boyish passion does not find an echo in her. For brief moments she feels some comfort in his embrace, but alternately senses it only as a restraining clutch. Consequently she quickly leaves for home.

Through the remainder of the fragment, Jutta's "perversion"

becomes evident and even her first homosexual experiences do not clear up her self-doubt. Through her brother, who has become a medical student, as well as through the rest of the Bamberger family, the hypocritical smugness of the society surrounding Jutta is strongly emphasized. The inane chatter of her sisters, the silly notions of her mother, and the double-faced superficiality of her father all serve to emphasize the contrast.

One of the few characters who first recognizes and uncritically accepts Jutta is Flavia Boscarolli, a mature woman who runs an establishment dedicated to providing exquisite sexual favors to a highly select group of fifty "founders," Jutta's father among them. In an angry encounter between the protective brother Karl and the incensed Flavia, the latter lectures the medical student on the facts of Jutta's life. Even though Karl is close to his sister, his bourgeois sensibility finds it extremely hard to accept the legitimacy of his sister's feelings. Only by repeatedly invoking the unfathomable forces of "life," which, he persuades himself, must be accepted *in toto*, can he come to any reconciliation.

After having been enlightened by Flavia, Karl decides to continue his studies elsewhere. The departure scene, like numerous scenes in this fragment, makes use of the metaphor of light, but in this instance the light is drastically reduced:

From his empty room the light falls onto the corridor. Jutta looks in front of herself into the dark and is seized by a sudden deep fear [*Grauen*]: as if she were falling away from all warmth and nearness, as if she were looking into outer space which was clanging [*klirrend*] with coldness. (FP, 172)

As in *Die Bresche*, overstatement, projecting small phenomena onto a nearly cosmic scale, and a hectic, abrupt style are telltale marks both of Doderer's youth and of Expressionism. This is true, of course, not only for the style but for the theme as well. The juxtaposition of insensitive parents and sensitive children and the conflicts generated by sexuality, are part of the stock in trade of Expressionism.

The first movement of the fragment ends with Jutta's loss of her first lover, Jekaterina Sofyanova. At this crisis point, in her seventeenth year, the fragment ends. The only other part remaining is the so-called "Episode f," which Doderer wrote prior to the first movement and in which Jutta appears only at the end. Here we once again meet S. A. Slobedeff in his role as liberator and wise, true-to-life master. This time he comes to the aid of a Russian expatriate poet, Vladimir Lancornin, who finds himself stuck and unable to

Beginnings and Resolve 41

pen a line. Slobedeff's way of breaking the "walled enclosure of his soul" involves a visit to Flavia Boscarolli's establishment. Lancornin serves as a foil to Jutta, because he too struggles with his tendency to be different in matters of sexuality.

Slobedeff delivers a long lecture to Lancornin on the need to accept life with all its contradictions, including one's internal conflicts. As in *Die Bresche*, the emphasis lies on recognition and acceptance of chaos or "house beasts" (*Hausbestien*): ". . . to recognize the existence of the 'house beasts,' quietly keeping your eye on them and to settle down with them somehow on the other side of the wall!" (FP, 194). Slobedeff's long sermon may be summed up in an aphorism which is frequently found in Doderer's diaries: "to think according to life, not to live according to thought." Slobedeff's sermon is, in fact, related to Doderer's insistence on honesty, love of truth, and a reality that includes the notion of evil. Doderer's vitalism is emphatically not amoral, but his treatment of evil differs from that found in other (German) writers: "Doderer does not demonize evil (as Thomas Mann in *Doctor Faustus*), but dedemonizes it by making it understandable."[29] In *Die Bresche* we are not dealing with evil, as in *Die Dämonen*, but rather with the conflict of sexual desires and societal norms. Doderer does not preach or sermonize from any particular viewpoint and resists, as always, the temptation to embrace any intellectual or moral ideology.

"Episode f" may be of interest because of the reappearance of Slobedeff, but what remains memorable in the entire fragment is the tender protrait of Jutta Bamberger and her brother Karl. Stylistically and emotionally youthful, the story seems to have been carefully planned and composed. Even the peripheral figures, such as Lancornin, although they seem to have no fate of their own, provide interesting contrasts to and support for the uniqueness and fullness of Jutta's character. Jutta's ability to "apperceive" is stressed by the leitmotif of "tunnel eyes" and the combination of metaphors of openness and light. Doderer continues to stress the need for apperception, which, as he is eager to point out, derives from the Latin *aperte percipere*, "to perceive openly." The opposite, the refusal to apperceive (*Apperceptions-Verweigerung*), becomes one of the deadly sins in Doderer's moral world. For these ideas Jutta Bamberger is an important early representative.[30]

IV *"Divertimenti" I through VI*

On September 13, 1923, Doderer made this entry in his diary: "Problems of prose narrative: actually this interests me more than anything at the present time; one thing I know for sure: the old techniques *won't do anymore*, and fifty years from now somebody will write in a way we can't even dream of today."[31] But two months later he already observes: "Today I think that theoretical examination doesn't help with the problem of prose narrative; anyway, one can surely become conscious of the guidelines (*Richtlinien*). Essential however: *intensive looking during writing*. The rules grow by themselves, from practice."[32] Constantly keeping a subject or a character in front of him, and intensively contemplating phenomena seemed to him to yield the best results.

In the diaries of the 1920's Doderer exhorts himself to produce; he almost flings commands at himself. We can also read observations concerning the task of writing, which become more developed in his later works: "What annoys me most of all is the servitude which places upon the novelist 'subject matter,' events, in brief: the story which has to be told."[33] It seems that Doderer wants to get the story out of the way, in order to concentrate on pure description. We can observe in the diaries the first stirrings of the kinds of stories and novels that do not have a simple, single story line, but are gradually built by a breaking away from and returning to narrative centers. Consequently, in the later works, the reader frequently feels that little happens in Doderer's stories. We can see that problems of content and form preoccupied Doderer from his earliest years as a writer, and that the idea of his last years, the "silent novel," the "roman muet," is already hinted at in Doderer's youth.

Often Doderer gives us a glimpse into the spiritual side of his thinking. In November 1923 he says: "Listen—don't make noise!" (*Lauschen, nicht lärmen!*). Reality (God) is so quiet that our foreground distorts it."[34] Here we recognize one essential feature of every positive Doderer character: the ability to listen intensely; to nothing in particular, to other people, to daydreams, or to structured thoughts. In short, they have "apperceptive" ability.

For Doderer as well as for his protagonists, it is much more important that people have "characteristics" that make them individuals than "convictions," "views," or "opinions."

"What matters is to remain close to the stream of life, not to get lost in side canals, not to stagnate in judgments, not to determine one's views, and not to decide and restrict oneself in external things: the only way to deal with these distractions is to counter them with notorious indifference."[35] We can see that Doderer reacts vehemently to any writing that moralizes or tries to convince the reader of the validity of an ideology.

Beginnings and Resolve

Nevertheless Doderer's own theories do not imply that he wrote only pure prose divorced from life. By 1926 he finished six Divertimenti and some short stories. "Divertimento No. I" portrays (against the background of the workers' riots which occurred on December 1, 1921 in Vienna) the relationship of a young man and a young woman, Adrian and Rufina. While Adrian lacks sensitivity, Rufina's hypersensitivity becomes pathological and finally drives her into a mental institution. But in spite of her illness she remains the heroine of the story, revealing through her fears and nightmares and intense self-castigation the shallowness of Adrian and of others who surround her, including the riotous masses.

Not unlike Jutta Bamberger, Rufina has eyes that are described as tunnels, and she is terribly distressed with what she sees, both inside and outside of herself. After she is confined to a mental institution, Adrian and a young psychologist discuss her case and the doctor explores the proximity of insanity and poetry, and the inadequacy of language, ignoring the immediacy of Rufina's problems. In a twist worthy of Arthur Schnitzler, the story ends with Adrian and a new girlfriend sitting in a charming terrace café, at night, looking over the city lights and raising their glasses to each other.

"Divertimento No. 2" addresses itself specifically to *listeners*. We are again introduced to a young man, thirty-five years old, married, with three children, and a successful business executive. The young man has arrived at a point in his life where contemplation of the past begins to outweigh concern for the future. Life, which is compared to a flowing river, something no one can hold onto, awes us suddenly with the certainty that there is nothing at all tentative about what has passed, that the past is fixed as permanently and firmly as a "rock in the mountain." Nevertheless, this "Divertimento" revolves around a precarious journey into the past.

While the family of Jaroslav Jentsch is vacationing in the countryside, the grass widower entertains himself in part by visiting friends in a Viennese café. (It is at this point, incidentally, that Stangeler, Doderer's alter ego, appears in print for the first time.) During the conversation somebody mentions the construction of a dam. It so happens that the water reservoir created by this dam will flood the house where Jentsch grew up. The remainder of the story describes his journey into scenes of his youth.

After arriving at the reservoir, Jentsch rents a boat and rows through the half-immersed village to the old house where he grew up. By chance he is soon joined by a woman whom he used to know quite well when he lived there. In an ecstatic mood he tells her that his love for her was "the true, the right, the only one."[36] Their chance meeting turns into a love affair of one night's duration. But in spite of the momentary passion, again and again the passage of time, their age, and their disillusionment intrude. Even during a passionate embrace, Jentsch thinks of the office. The morning after, they part with great sadness, each drifting off in a different direction in a rowboat, a feeling of evanescence, of mortality, and of ennui pervading the atmosphere. Both are caught in a prosaic existence, and, like all of us, are unable to resist or halt the flow of time, or to stop the instrusion of consciousness.

"Divertimento No. 3" can be read as the depiction of one man's inability to come to terms with the chaotic forces of life. After his wife has died in childbirth, Fedor Wittasek is left with a daughter. The initial mourning and desperate sadness prevent him from accepting his daughter Lily, but after she suffers a severe illness the wall is broken and father and daughter establish an affectionate relationship. However, the routine and the order of Wittasek's life leave him deeply dissatisfied, and when the affection of his daughter is directed towards young men of her age, Wittasek, in a fit of jealousy, accuses her of having killed her mother. Almost immediately thereafter he admits to himself that he is in love with his daughter. Wittasek's world is thoroughly confused, and as one who has surrounded his life with painstaking order this realization nearly shatters him.

The "cure" comes from a chance meeting with a woman whom Wittasek used to know, and whom he will eventually marry. The scientist and researcher who has dedicated his career to discovering the subtlest and smallest physical phenomena has been blind with respect to his own emotions, and in the end, Wittasek must come to an uncritical acceptance of the complexity of life. Doderer again juxtaposes the more instinctual and, hence, wiser woman with the cerebral and, hence, more stupid man. The story also emphasized the paradox between the microscope-aided investigations of Wittasek which exclude, in their specialization, important aspects of life, and the spontaneous ability to apperceive which distinguishes the "female, looking with dark eyes" (E, 66).

Stylistically and thematically, this "Divertimento" bears marks of typical Expressionistic prose, with lyrical outbursts, impatient, rapid narration, and violent imagery ("wild, and like an animal that has been stepped on, the pain screams out, it glows around the outlines which have returned—scintillating—from eternity, around this greeting which files the heart to pieces") (E, 67). Exclamations

Beginnings and Resolve

beginning with "'Oh . . .'" abound, and a high degree of pathos underlies this "Divertimento." In this instance, there are none of Doderer's interjections, authorial interventions, or breaks in the narrative viewpoint which lend objectivity and lightheartedness to so many of his other stories.

"Divertimento No. 4" is important not only because, according to his diary, Doderer found the work on it helpful during a personal crisis, but also because it seems to have been the first which Doderer recited to an audience completely from memory. Even though it stretches the length of the Divertimento form to an extreme, it was apparently a successful recitation which took place on March 16, 1927. Doderer had begun memorizing it on December 1, of the previous year. He triumphantly notes that he had thereby proven that his theories concerning the Divertimento as oral literature had once and for all been proven right.[37] Beginning with the contrast of country-city, this "Divertimento" opens with the long invocation of the misery of modern industrial-urban life. Doderer refers to the "dull compulsion of our age" which moves on iron tracks and "plows a glorious alley through masses of bleeding hearts" (E, 91). Out of the screaming factory sirens, the smoke, and the masses of people emerges a young man named Adam who hurries to work one morning, but as he is jumping on the bus, he falls and faints. The main portion of the Divertimento takes place in Adam's fantasies and dreams during his unconscious state. He dreams that he finds himself on an island from which he can see the city. But some disaster has taken place, because the city is destroyed and, initially, Adam is alone on the island. Through the dream Doderer places him in a situation where civilized concerns do not matter and the central ones do, such as the task of finding food. After some time, a group of men and women arrive in boats and soon Adam becomes the patriarch of a peaceful agricultural commune.

The peace is disrupted by the arrival of another group consisting of men only who, unlike Adam, have pretenses of being rescuers of civilization. What Adam perceives as leading in the end to suffering, industrialization, and enslavement is to the newcomers the crown of human achievement. Conflict between the two groups becomes inevitable, and it leads in the end to combat and the death of the intruders. After peace is restored, Adam gradually awakes from his dream. This "Divertimento," full of action, drama, love, and adventure, can be read as a recapitulation of human history. Although Adam perceives the destructive nature of civilization, he cannot stop human inventiveness: a little boy designs a crossbow, and from this point on the development of progressively more destructive weapons is merely a matter of time. The murderous nature of man will assert itself.

"Divertimento No. 5" begins with general observations. Among them we find some of the key symbols of this story: ". . . We drift on the surface with all our affairs, like a blanket of autumn leaves drifting on the surface of a pond. . ." (E, 129). With this image Doderer suggests that we are seldom aware of the depths within us. If a single gesture would have to be found that expresses the theme of this story it would be that of "letting go." Behaving like fish caught in a net, our restlessness only hastens our doom: "Better, let go, if you are confused, let go and lie and breathe—but who can do that? No, we twist and turn in the net" (E, 129).

Twisting and turning is precisely what the protagonist of the story, the lawyer Georg, does. A sudden, accidental event brings the hero to a crisis, to the proximity of death, and through intervention of an arbitrary fate he is tested. He will then either perish or emerge as a different human being. Thus, the events of this Divertimento conform to similar schemes in Doderer's work.

Georg arises one morning, and during that day nothing goes right. Like many Doderer characters, he is gifted with a sensitive nose, and certain smells, especially vinegary ones, tend to annoy him. These repulsive smells abound on this particular day. After rushing and muddling through the work day, he practically runs through the streets of the city, and as the first movement ends, Georg is hit by a bus. In the hospital, Georg gradually drifts back into consciousness and in a dreamlike, drugged state, his imagination surrounds him with sensations of pleasant, clean, good-smelling things. The enforced rest compels him to a degree of contemplation that has a healing effect on him. Images of lightness and translucence surround him, and, like in other, earlier works, Doderer sometimes breaks into lyrical prose passages and even lines of verse at the end of two sections of the "Divertimento."

During Georg's absence from his job and his affairs, all of his problems seem to arrange or solve themselves; where once he has seen thorny difficulties, simple and amicable solutions emerge. Georg's attempts at solving problems and at manipulating people are not half as successful as his enforced "letting go." During his stay in the hospital, he rediscovers simple things. More importantly, he rediscovers his own ability to observe the undistorted world and finds a renewed capacity simply to move around, to sit, and to see, in an unhurried, quiet way. In terms of the symbolism of this story,

Georg has emptied himself, and now the sensations can flow into him without interference from his busy mind. He has learned to feel, and as frequently happens in Doderer's stories, he briefly escapes from the city to the surrounding countryside and its pleasant sights and smells. Even the body's motion during his walk through the "red autumn" helps Georg to clear his mind. As an echo or a development of the symbolism of the drifting leaves on the surface, we read in the end: "Georg stood as if seized by a remembrance . . .he sank and forgot himself a little: spring and autumn, where was I, why not diving deeper, joining the rising and sinking—. . ." (E, 142).

Aside from the characteristic story line, the olfactory sensitivity of the hero, the expedition into the healing countryside, and the implied flight from the industrious-urban scene, Georg discovers another aspect of his mind which he has previously neglected: the capacity to remember. In developing this faculty, he foreshadows other Doderer characters, particularly Melzer in *Die Strudlhofstiege*. The power of memory, not necessarily aimed at specific past events, extends and broadens the world in which the protagonists live. The spontaneity, the technique of letting something happen, of not willing or manipulating things, becomes important. No matter what emerges in our memory, it is the capacity that distinguishes the *Mensch* from the supernumerary character. Doderer describes the point where Georg changes in the following terms:

. . .A small, brief emptiness formed within him—for a moment he felt it this way: what mattered now was to let go, to open one's hands willingly, to let go of a small possession of importance, which wasn't one anyway, which had proven to be childish and nothing—and now to switch over quickly and humbly, without argument or much ado. . . . (E, 140)

The gesture of the open hands, of letting go, is associated with the entry of past events into our consciousness, and in Doderer's repertoire of metaphors is most clearly associated with memory. How important the function of memory is to Doderer can be seen from a later aphorism: "One would only have to remember properly and one would be a poet [*Dichter*]."[38]

The sixth "Divertimento," completed in 1926, was to be the last of these early experiments. Only in 1951 did Doderer return to this particular literary genre of his own making. Divertimento No. 6 also begins with an observation of a general nature. Doderer contrasts the mindless and hurried life with an existence where room is given to subtler perceptions, where the aura of a place is felt, where our senses, particularly that of smell, are not overwhelmed with the hectic demands of "busyness." In what appears to be a "blessed garden," outside of the city, there lives a young couple who has a child, named Victoria, who has been born blind. Of course, Victoria develops an exceptionally fine sense of hearing. *Victoria lauschte* ("Victoria listened intensely") becomes the leitmotif sentence of this story and is coupled with a striking image of inexorable fate: "Because what must come and must happen, plows through all the buildings of our heart. No veil can for long hide the angular [*kantige*] mask of fate: it steps through, tears, cuts the disguises again and again" (E, 144).

Little happens during Victoria's youth. She will, at any rate, become sighted during her tenth year of life and become a successful concert pianist. The content is not what makes the Divertimento interesting. Rather, the sustained description of the world of a young girl through aural imagery and sensations constitutes a verbal showpiece for Doderer. The nuances and the richness of a world that is heard and not seen result in a lyricism of which Doderer—the prose writer—is a consummate master. Into this wealth of heard images suddenly falls the light, as Victoria begins to see: "Then the storm wakened, the belated morning arose in this child's life, accompanied by a tremendous uproar of light [*ungeheures Lichtgetöse*]" (E, 150).

The rich and confusing onrush of sight diverts Victoria's capacity to listen. For a while her life becomes shallower. But shortly before her twenty-third birthday she rediscovers the ability to listen inside herself and, through the power of aural memory, recalls the sounds of her childhood. Doderer stresses a particular kind of memory, the power to extend oneself into one's own past, and to survey the depths of past time. In his view, memory is a prerequisite for realizing our potential as human beings and thus for the process of humanization.

CHAPTER 2

Turning Point

I *Gütersloh as Doderer's Teacher*

AFTER writing numerous articles on history and the arts for various newspapers in Vienna in the late 1920s,[1] Doderer encountered in 1929 Paris von Gütersloh's *Bekenntnisse eines modernen Malers* (Confessions of a Modern Painter, publ. 1926).[2] He considered the reading of this autobiography a "turning point in his evolution as a writer."[3] Since his days in the POW camp in Siberia, Doderer had known and admired Gütersloh's work; he had met him personally in 1924, and then in 1929 he was commissioned by his first publisher to write a monograph on him.

The "Confessions" are heady reading. In very personal style and with sweeping intellectual gestures Gütersloh traces the development of the arts in general and of the artist (himself) in particular. He alludes to his views as anti-Puritan, anti-Marxist, anti-Gnostic, anti-Hegelian, and occasionally antidemocratic. He attempts to balance the conviction that art has no social value or function and that tragedy or high seriousness cannot be separated from cult (Bek, 90) with the reality of his life spent writing and painting. One of Gütersloh's ways to reconcile art without function and the very real existence of a serious artist is through a series of quasi-religious gestures. On the most obvious level the artist is asked to accept a certain degree of poverty: "In a certain sense, when I painted or wrote prose, I dressed in the cowl of a begging monk, and I let myself be paid with alms for the courage to live in voluntary poverty" (Bek, 18).

Gütersloh also perceives the necessity of justifying the fact that he does not simply seek refuge in established religious ceremony. He does this by asserting that he is ". . .not tied to a religion, but yet sees [*schaut*] religiously. . ." (Bek, 98). His views include belief in the historicity and divinity of Christ, a deep philosophical acceptance of the world as good and the feeling that mankind cannot live without the symbol of an eternal power: "For mankind cannot for a moment be without the symbol of a power established in eternity, which cannot be flattered by any merit. . ." (Bek, 123 - 24).

Gütersloh's apodictic assertions, his esoteric style occasionally puncturing its own high seriousness with slightly bawdy imagery,[4] reverberated in the mind of Doderer for a long time. At the time of Doderer's first reading of the "Confessions" he was still searching, still somewhat unsure of himself and his task in life. Doderer had suddenly found a sympathetic teacher-figure who stressed the development of one's own personality as one of the central duties of the artist, as well as the duty to live under and accept a variety of external circumstances, and the possibility of a "second birth," becoming a person. The idea that someone may change fundamentally is shared by Doderer and Gütersloh, and is seen as "the final goal of life" (Bek, 128).

A phrase from Gütersloh—who spent considerable effort in elucidating the teacher-student relationship as it applies to the artist—may shed some light on the affinity Doderer discovered with Gütersloh: ". . . the teacher, who stands up and defends life rigorously against any chiliastic hope. . ."·(Bek, 128). The chiliastic hope for the millennium after the second coming of Christ may be interpreted in this context as the tendency (characteristic of all ideologies) to consider the world in its present state as inferior to some postulated state in the future. Gütersloh and Doderer, on the other hand, stress the importance of accepting the here and now as valid and real, in their scholastic mannerism frequently using the Latin *hic et nunc*, words which even appear on Doderer's gravestone.

Two other ideas that were to become very important for Doderer originated with Gütersloh: the theory of the so-called "total novel," and the implications of Gütersloh's epithet "the depth is outside" (*die Tiefe ist aussen*). The ideas implicit in the concept of the total novel represent a development of theories inherent in German Naturalism. Attempting a painstakingly accurate depiction of reality in their writings, the Naturalists soon reached an aesthetic impasse, because the distinctions between art and life became blurred and finally nonexistent. As Doderer remarks sarcastically, novels in the form of "newspapers between hard covers" are the end result of Naturalism.

The total novel Doderer would attempt to write seeks a compromise between all-inclusiveness and aesthetic selection. Nevertheless it would accommodate the conjunction of phenomena

Turning Point 51

in a way that doesn't "make sense": "The [total novel] doesn't attempt to integrate the meaningless at all costs by giving it meaning."[5] Thus the relationship of the concept of the total novel is probably closer to the theories of Surrealism than to Naturalism.

The total novel—like any novel—may have more than one theme. It attempts, however, to treat several actions, themes, or characters with equal emphasis. To illustrate his intentions, Doderer uses the image of two chains that may at times touch, at times intertwine. Neither chain is necessarily more important than any other: "In the total novel there are no main voices and accompanying voices, even less than in polyphony, which still tries to 'get somewhere.' "[6] The polycentric novels, *Die Strudlhofstiege* and *Die Dämonen*, will be better understood if these theoretical deliberations are considered.

It should be emphasized at the same time that Doderer's theories parallel rather than dictate his novelistic practice, and that Doderer has a penchant for striking formulations and images even in his essays on theory. The perception of the ideal total novel is, for example, described in the following manner: "The total novel should see the world with almost glassy eyes, which will soon break and turn upward, and which will soon reflect only the empty sky. But this moment of farewell, where one is still entirely here, but no longer wants anything, this moment would have to make us perceptive in a most unique way."[7] The image of the eye at the point of death, the vision made possible by the absence of will (volition), and the idea of letting the images of the world enter a passive consciousness remind us of the blend of mystical notions Doderer seems to favor.

Gütersloh's dictum "the depth is outside" also stresses the importance of real, exterior, and tangible phenomena, rather than flights into presumed depths of the human soul. In accepting Gütersloh's dictum Doderer takes a polemical stance against what he saw as the tendency of German novels to focus on realms of the psyche, to write nonrealistic, or as he calls them "transreal" novels. In opposition to the perhaps typically German notion of *Innerlichkeit*, or of the depths of inwardness, Doderer asserts the value and importance of the surface-world for the creative writer. Hence the smells emanating from a Danube canal may equal in importance profound observations on medieval historiography. To be sure, it must be added that, after all, the depth is not outside, but in Doderer's rich imagination, his tolerance, his sensitivity, all resulting in a unique and—for German literature, at least—rare solidity of specification.

A third idea might be added to the main foci of Gütersloh's influence. Doderer pinpoints it by a principle derived from Medieval

Scholasticism, *operari sequitur esse,* translated by him as "our actions (and thus our work) come from our being."[8] Gütersloh provided a unique example of dedication to the craft of writing and painting. While one must be careful not to interpret the scholastic principle of the primacy of being over work in a shallow manner, there were some pedestrian implications for Doderer. He did, for example, believe in the necessity of working harder, getting up earlier, and working later than the ordinary "bourgeois," and he did shy away from any outward suggestion of a bohemian life-style, or of clever, businesslike assessment of literary tastes and trends, and any attempt to write to sell well.

In a manner reminiscent of Schiller, Doderer looks back to earlier cultures, particularly to ancient Greece, where "action continuously flows from being" (WdD, 67), where a unity of cult and culture still existed, where legitimate works of art proceeded from a spiritual core. To clarify his idea, Doderer uses the image of the body as the spiritual center, with the arts pictured as smoothly fitting clothes. The development of Western art—one is reminded of his reading of Spengler—is seen as the decline and eventual death of the body, and the mysterious stiffening of the clothes, until the resulting image is that of a suit of armor encasing a dead body. Balancing this macabre image Doderer tends to see artists, who successfully produce and market their wares, more forgivingly as *gamins de génie,* naughty geniuses, unprincipled but street-wise, who produce *original-echt amerikanisches Tempo* (WdD, 70).

II Das Geheimnis des Reiches
(The Mystery of the Kingdom)

Das Geheimnis des Reiches—the title borrowed from the closing words of Gerhart Hauptmann's novel *Der Narr in Christo Emanuel Quint*—is largely based on Doderer's experiences in Siberia. The novel describes the turmoil, intrigues, brutality, as well as the civilized aspect of life in the camps; the struggle of the "Reds" and the "Whites," and the final escape of two of the protagonists, Alwersik and René Stangeler, to Vienna. Doderer interweaves (auto-) biographical and historical content. In spite of the brutality of the Revolution, the instant executions, and the murderous nature of (Communist) ideology, the underlying "mystery" or "secret" (*Geheimnis* can mean either) of the Russian "kingdom" prevails. It was Doderer's experience that the kingdom is constituted by the unshakably humane concerns of the Russian peasants who help the young Austrian officers during their escape by sharing bread, milk,

Turning Point

and scriptural truths with them. The mystery is inherent in the expanse of the Russian landscape, and, as we have seen previously in *Die Bresche*, landscape and human fate are inexplicably intertwined.

Das Geheimnis des Reiches is Doderer's first attempt at polygraphic or panoramic composition.[9] Because Doderer originally planned it as another "Divertimento," the novel is divided into four parts; but unlike the shorter "Divertimenti," each part is subdivided into small episodes. These episodes follow each other rapidly, and at first the reader is unaware of the connection between each. The switch may occur from one paragraph to the next, and thus no clear narrative center is established. Hence, the single authorial viewpoint on which readers comfortably rely is absent. One slowly discovers the connections existing between the various episodes and characters; and this process of gradual revelation, comparable to a detective novel without suspense can be followed with a great deal of enjoyment.

In *Das Geheimnis des Reiches* as well as in "Jutta Bamberger," Doderer was faced with the problem of reconciling a new form with a more or less traditional content. The episodic composition is obscured by the story of the love triangle of Dorian, Alwersik, and Katjä which gradually absorbs more and more of our interest, so that other episodes seem to fade into the background. The historical events, particularly the approach of the Red Army, seem to possess a dynamism of their own which does not lend itself very well to episodic treatment. It is not the historical events per se that resist such compositional technique but rather the "realistic" history-book treatment of the subject which detracts from attempts to break up the narration. Doderer had not yet found his own, personal, and possibly eccentric, way of treating history. In this novel, history emerges as historiography, complete with statistics, historical figures, and excerpts from Lenin's speeches. In subsequent novels, particularly in *Die Dämonen*, Doderer attempts to step behind historiography and portray the evolution of historical time and events in a more indirect and human manner.

Nevertheless, this first attempt at episodic composition contains masterfully lyrical descriptions of the aura of the Siberian landscape and the changing seasons, as well as glimpses into key events of Doderer's life. The sounds, smells, the very atmosphere of the battle of Olesza, where Doderer was captured, emerge with vivid clarity; and the period of his life as a lumberjack—including an episode where Doderer's alter ego René Stangeler is severely wounded by an axe—is described with sensitivity and lyricism.

It also becomes clear that Doderer considers these years of enforced absence from the urban turmoil and the resultant enforced period of contemplation as the fountainhead of his writing. Like his capture, his career began quite accidentally: "He, Stangeler, had discovered, while drifting off to sleep, that he was working with a basic mistake: it became crystal-clear to him that only the distance from his entire earlier, dull life, a distance which had been created involuntarily, as an external event—that only this distance. . .had created the illusion of the possibility of liberation, development, salvation, that all his writing [Schreiberei] was only a product of external chance, tied to this, and that life in the camp was crazy and completely extraordinary" (FP, 265). Stangeler, like Doderer, accepts the direction into which the "external events" of his life have pushed him. Doderer would never stray far from his vocation as a writer, and the beginnings in Russia were to remain a source of inspiration to him.

III Smaller Prose Works of the 1930s

During the 1930s Doderer completed a number of stories, among them the final version of *Das letzte Abenteuer* (The Last Adventure, pub. 1953), *Die Peinigung der Lederbeutelchen* (The Torment of the Leather Pouches, pub. 1959) and *Zwei Lügen oder Eine antike Tragödie auf dem Dorfe* (Two Lies, or: Classical Tragedy in a Village, pub. 1972). Some of these short prose pieces are one-paragraph vignettes. Toward the end of this decade, Doderer also finished the "Ouverture" to *Die Dämonen* (1935), and, in part while in lodgings in Dachau, *Ein Mord den jeder begeht* (Every Man a Murderer, pub. 1938). He also completed the short novel *Ein Umweg* (A Detour, pub. 1940) and *Die erleuchteten Fenster oder Die Menschwerdung des Amstrates Julius Zihal* (The Illuminated Windows, or: The Humanization of Councillor Julius Zihal, pub. 1950).

During that same decade, Doderer also married, and was divorced from, Gusti Hasterlik, joined and then became disenchanted with the illegal National Socialist party in Vienna, found a publisher (C. H. Beck, later Biederstein), met—in a circus—Maria Emma Thoma, whom he married after the war, and wrote a cycle of poems inspired by Baudelaire. In 1940, as an emphatic gesture to mark the distance between himself and the prevailing ideology, he converted to Catholicism, even though his family had been Protestant for generations.

Despite the turmoil in his life, the 1930s were productive years for

Doderer. The short stories, and shortest stories (*Kurzgeschichten* and *Kürzestgeschichten*), and stories (*Erzählungen*) he wrote then number around two dozen.[10] Many are humorous or grotesque, sometimes depicting inexplicable events. One even is told from the "point of view" of a dog. Some contain sketches of characters that would appear again in his works. Karoline in "The Amputation," like Mary K. of *Die Strudlhofstiege* and *Die Dämonen*, has lost one leg and been fitted with an artificial one in a famous clinic in Munich. Some of the stories could be called tales of the supernatural. In "The Gulf of Naples," a person enters an amusement park, visits a "scare" ride, nearly gets lost inside, and only barely escapes. Others abound with Doderer's often biting humor. In "The Alley of Compassion," a young woman, whose mother has just died, finds herself unable to function adequately because the rest of the world does not seem to share her grief. One day, she observes a group of people crying in the street. She is so amazed and moved by this inexplicable display of communal grief that she begins to adjust to her plight. To be sure, she soon discovers that the abundance of tears had been caused by an accidental spill of a large quantity of ammonia, but the salutary effect of the original "vision" remains with her nevertheless.

Begegnung im Morgengrauen (Encounter at Dawn) is a vivid illustration of Doderer's penchant for the slightly grotesque, as well as for his portrayal of chance encounters which are surprisingly meaningful. The story takes place in January 1916, in the middle of the First World War, and describes the meeting in a train compartment of a young officer returning to the trenches of the Western Front with a well-dressed man who turns out to be an executioner on his way to a "job" in Cologne. The story begins with the young officer's arrival at a railroad station, between two and three o'clock in the morning, after an evening of "celebrating" his departure with ample libations. His friends, who are recuperating from wounds received in battle, complain about the dull life on the "homefront" and express their envy of Herr von E. who is going into "action." Doderer recreates with great economy the atmosphere of the slightly embarrassed departure. The soldiers seem to be alone on the dull, soot-covered station, while snatches of their conversation reveal the bored and superficial life of the young officers.

The express train starts suddenly but quietly and transports Herr von E. into the darkness of the countryside and into an uncertain future. As he falls into his seat, exhausted and slightly drunk, he suddenly notices that he is sharing the compartment with a man whom he instantly judges to be from Saxony, an exceptional even-tempered *gemütlicher Sachse*. To be sure, his look and posture seem to be the opposite of *gemütlich*. At three o'clock in the morning he sits at the window, "squat, upright and straight" (*breit, aufrecht und gerade*). He is dressed "correctly," with a standing collar that makes him look somewhat like a priest. The stranger turns out to be from Kottbus and speaks a relaxed Saxony dialect that Doderer recreates with notable accuracy.

Herr von E. spies a long black case in the luggage rack above his companion and hastily concludes that the gentleman is a trombonist. A string of associations lead him to the "trumpets of judgment day" (*eine Posaune des jüngsten Gerichts*), which turns out to be grotesquely correct, since the "instrument" is the executioner's axe. Herr von E.'s somewhat befogged mind quickly becomes alert when the "Saxon" nonchalantly says: "That's an executioner's axe, up there (*Das is'n Richtbeil, da oben*) (E, 256). Eager to accommodate and demonstrate, the executioner opens the red velvet-lined case containing the heavy axe which, like a precious violin, is wrapped in white silk. In fact, the Saxon does play the violin back home in Kottbus. Lifting the mercury-filled blade, Herr von E. stammers: "Well, I'll be.—Did you ever. . .with this. . .?" (*Deibel noch mal.-Ham' Se mit dem da schon—?*) (E, 257).

Prim and proper, the executioner descends from the train in Cologne while Herr von E. continues on his way to the front. The train needs to overcome a considerable incline and therefore a second locomotive is added, thus both pulling and shoving Herr von E. In his dreamlike state, he is plagued by notions of impending disaster, including the obsession that something is pushing itself between his head and his heart. At the very point where the train reaches the top of the incline and begins to glide effortlessly along, Herr von E. checks his wristwatch and realizes that at precisely this time the executioner's axe is falling on its victim's neck. Curiously relieved—perhaps because someone else has had to die—Herr von E. leans back, and, dreaming pleasant dreams, is transported to what might well be his own death.

Upon a closer look at the story, we discover that it follows the scheme of many Doderer narratives: some chance event intrudes unexpectedly into the protagonist's life, throws him or her abruptly off the tracks of a comfortable previous existence, thus testing the value of the protagonist's character. In many instances, the event represents a challenge which, if it were taken up, might add a new dimension to the life of the protagonist; or, to use Doderer's term, a

Turning Point

step may be taken in the direction of humanization. The favored image of the railroad tracks functions in a familiar way in *Begegnung im Morgengrauen*. Against the backdrop of the war, the young officer gentleman remains "tracked," and even the encounter with symbolic death fails to "derail" him from his comfortable and predictable existence. Seen in these terms, the train's overcoming of the incline while the young officer is haunted by disturbing dreams, could be interpreted as an unconscious attempt to integrate the encounter with death into his existence. But no such integration takes place, since Herr von E. feels "infinitely relieved" when the train reaches the top of the hill, the exact moment when the executioner's axe is falling on the neck of the victim. After that point, the train has overcome the strain of the incline, and the young officer seems to have overcome as well whatever conflict has briefly plagued him. Because someone else was the victim, he remains in his comfortable soldierly attitude understandably ignoring the threat of death, and at the same time moving smoothly and quietly closer to his death.

Among ths nongrotesque, nonhumorous, nonflippant stories, *Zwei Lügen oder eine antikische Tragödie auf dem Dorfe* (Two Lies, or: Classical Tragedy in a Village)[11] is remarkable for its intense treatment of a folkloristic theme variously known as "the son's fatal homecoming," *Mordeltern*, or *le fils assassiné*. An older son returns, unrecognized, to his parents after an absence of almost eighteen years. (Not coincidentally, the long-lost son has been in Siberia and is thirty-six years old, Doderer's age at the time of the writing of this story.) The son has become rich and is now able to relieve the poverty of his parents. He does not reveal his identity to them, and they, driven by poverty and greed, murder him for his money. In Doderer's version, the actual killing is done by the mother and the younger brother. The father goes to the village inn for a drink. While sitting among the villagers, he is informed by them that his son has returned, and that he was asking earlier about his parents. The father denies that anyone has been at their house. Upon returning home, he finds the mother and the younger son alreadying counting the murdered son's money. Discovery and punishment follow swiftly, the entire action taking only a few hours.

Even though he has told the first lie at the village inn, the father now is transformed from a somewhat weak and clumsy peasant into an active and assured avenger, who directs the subsequent steps of the action. He even prepares the rope for his wife's suicide, making it quite clear to her what she is to do. He lays out his dead son, prays over him, instructs the younger son to go to his room and not to tell anyone that he has heard or seen anything. Returning to the inn for a second time, he confesses his deed, although he now tells a second lie: that he and his wife killed the son and that the younger son is completely innocent. He feels redeemed, collapses, and dies.

Even though the peasant father achieves a certain stature as an avenger, and even though one might read the story as an archetypal conflict between parents and children, "Zwei Lügen" remains, first of all, a well-told story, well planned by Doderer in his diary, where he graphically traced the progress of the tension.[12] Having aspects of a folktale, the story also thrives because of Doderer's masterful handling of the sometimes sparse, sometimes formalized dialogue, and because of the striking images that are Doderer's trademark: the gold on the kitchen table compared to a continuously exploding grenade. As in the "Divertimenti," content and meaning recede behind the primacy of form and language; consequently, the story appears to be almost an exercise, albeit consummately composed.

Herbert Knust has examined "Zwei Lügen" in some detail, comparing it with Albert Camus's *Le Malentendu*.[13] He points out that, in contrast to Camus's play, Doderer's novella implies reintegration into a moral order, inasmuch as after the murder the father "reenters the village community, subjecting himself to the principles by which it is governed."[14] It is also important to note that the fatal outcome of the action is, in part, caused by deficient perception. While mother and father do not recognize their son, an old woman, named Dablenka, recognizes him when he enters the village. (Interestingly, the real mother in the story is never given a name, and she remains the unredeemed villain.) Even though Doderer was dealing with a traditional, folkloristic theme, the problem of a failure of recognition, or failure of perception (*Apperzeption*), even though it has aspects of an accident rather than intention, must have attracted him. The almost ceremonious walks of the father to and from the house to the village give Doderer the opportunity of illustrating the processes of sinning (walking away from the house), discovery (the slow walk back) and redemption (the final walk into the village).

The walks are not, as Knust maintains, a good illustration of Doderer's notion of the "indirect" or the *Umweg* which asserts that the process of full apperception, or cognition, is usually circuitous or indirect, and that it is frequently necessary to step back, in order to come close to a problem. In "Zwei Lügen" each walk represents the simple connection between the stages in the development in the story which culminates in the acceptance of a moral order. Frequently, as in Doderer's later novels *Ein Umweg* and *Ein Mord den*

Turning Point

jeder begeht, recognition or acceptance of incomprehensible fate represents the only positive outcome.

This is not the case with "Zwei Lügen". We do not know the moral stature of the father before the inception of the action, although we can assume that the domineering and hard mother has prevailed. Thus the change in the nature of the father, his sudden development into a character of some tragic stature, intent on discovering the truth even though it may destroy him, is an instance of anagnoresis and peripeteia. In the two novels cited, the "detour," the process of indirect approach, is represented by the plot. Once the hero recognizes that he went a long way to traverse a short distance, the action is practically completed and he speeds to his doom. In "Zwei Lügen," the recognition occurs rather early in the story and is followed by a righting of wrongs to the extent that the finality of death permits such righting.

The story to be discussed next differs from the sombre "Zwei Lügen" in theme and style. "Die Peinigung der Lederbeutelchen" features two of the most amiable and crotchety eccentrics among Doderer's characters, Mr. Coyle and Mr. Crotter. J. A. Palma Caetano considers the story one of Doderer's most original.[15] The British setting distinguishes it from most of the others, and, true to the stereotype of the mercantile English, the story features the old miser, Mr. Coyle, and his relationship with his only and equally rich friend Mr. Crotter. After the death of Mr. Coyle, Mr. Crotter goes to visit his attorney, who functions as the rather passive narrator listening to the ludicrous obsessions of Mr. Crotter with growing amazement and, finally, impatience. It is revealed in these "confessions"—Crotter dismisses the possibility of seeing a clergyman—that Mr. Crotter is the only person who has seen the treasures of Mr. Coyle which consists of thirty-six suede leather pouches, each containing precious stones or gold nuggets. The pouches are numbered and kept in a velvet-lined chest. The sight of these pouches deeply offends Mr. Crotter, whose imagination transforms them into disgusting, squat, spiteful little dwarfs whom he is determined to "punish." Having taken instructions in techniques of burglary, he enters Mr. Coyle's house at night, gains access to the chest, and disarranges the sequence of the leather pouches, thereby "torturing the 'little fellows.'"

Mr. Crotter relates that after each torment he expected Mr. Coyle to fly into a rage, but nothing of the sort happened. The old miser was apparently intent on not letting his friend see the repercussions of his actions. Mr. Crotter protests to the lawyer that none of his actions have been aimed at his old friend but merely at the disgusting little fellows. Through a ludicrous twist, the "truth" is at least partially revealed. Mr. Crotter had devised a particular punishment for pouch seventeen, suspending "him" outside the window during a cold night. At the end of the confession, a clerk delivers a letter from the late Mr. Coyle to his friend, which contains the empty pouch seventeen with a strip of paper stuck in its mouth, on which is written: "I am cold. I am getting very cold. . ." (E, 361). Mr. Crotter takes final revenge on the "miserable grey-belly," tossing him into the open fire. At the same time, he realizes that Mr. Coyle must have been fully aware of his own compulsive games but has preferred to remain quiet. Mr. Coyle had thus proven his superiority and, in a violent outburst directed at his lawyer, Mr. Crotter's hostility is finally directed against its valid target, his late friend. The lawyer, at the end of his patience, remains stubbornly unsympathetic to Mr. Crotter's imagined plight and, as a consequence, he will lose in the near future the lucrative Crotter account.

In the end, we realize that Mr. Crotter, who holds the notion of order in highest regard, has been transferring his hatred for the slovenly miser to his clean and orderly riches. The alleged torment consists largely of ritualistic but harmless disordering of the normally sequential arrangement of the pouches. Crotter naturally assumes that any disturbance of this order would have to be experienced, as it is by him, as nearly physical torment. In his obsession with order, Mr. Crotter foreshadows Julius Zihal of the later novels.

"Die Peinigung der Lederbeutelchen" furnishes but one example of Doderer's portrayal of eccentricities, private obsessions, and inexplicable outbursts of violent anger. Most of the narratives of this kind date from the 1950s and 1960s and culminate in the humorous-grotesque novel *Die Merowinger oder Die totale Familie* (The Merovingians or The Total Family, 1962).

Doderer takes delight in portraying irrational or inexplicable actions that lead to serious confusions and destroy normal perceptions, including such fundamental distinctions as those between the animate and inanimate realms. Doderer's fools who are caught in the dilemmas are unashamedly outrageous; they are not buffoons, however, and sometimes the reader chokes on his laughter. While Doderer resisted any attempts at highly serious interpretations of his humorous novels, they represent the closest he ever came to the portrayal of the Absurd, although his religiosity prevented him from embracing such a notion.

The grotesque shades over into the macabre in Doderer's story

"Eine Person von Porzellan" (1935). A dainty lady sits in a Viennese café, leafing through the latest fashion magazines, making sketches and taking notes with a small golden pencil. She is "a small, severe, and exceedingly dainty goddess of well-ordered existence" (E, 306). When she leaves the café, the narrator follows her, fascinated. She makes her way to a big house in the suburbs, and, to the narrator's extreme disgust, is soon observed sitting in the corner of a large room, hacking and tearing at human corpses and feeding upon their flesh while uttering grunting, squeaking, and moaning noises. The appearance of gentility has given way to the disgusting reality of her life. Somehow relieved, the narrator reflects that he can accept the deranged activity of the woman, whereas the image of the lifeless, pure, and clean "goddess" would have haunted him forever.

Here, as well as in subsequent works, Doderer portrays the irrational, sometimes evil aspects of our world. It is characteristic for him to withhold obvious judgment of human behavior. Part of what he saw as his duty as a novelist was acceptance of human behavior which runs the gamut from bestial to sublime. Doderer has a warm spot for the eccentric, and even the criminal is occasionally admired. Instinctively suspicious of ideologues, he repeatedly asserts the primacy of the individual and the legitimacy of individual destiny which is found not in the collective, but rather in personal relationships, frequently one-to-one. However, the relationship is valid only *after* the individual has developed his own potential, or realized his own *Menschwerdung*.

IV *Fairytale or Realism:*
Das letzte Abenteuer *and* Ein Umweg

In spite of his wide reading and thorough familiarity with literary history, Doderer preferred slightly esoteric usage of standard literary terms. Thus his idea of Naturalism, although nurtured by Stendhal, Balzac, Zola, and Dostoyevsky, by no means designates a past period of literature, but rather a basic attitude of the novelist, which he also refers to as Realism or even as Impressionism. What mattered to Doderer was the idea of being "open" to the world that is portrayed. It seems therefore consonant with his naturalism that he would venture into distant times or places as the background for some of his stories. One of these ventures resulted in the long story *Das letzte Abenteuer*, which Doderer originally wrote in 1917, revised in 1923, and which now exists in a third version, written in 1936 but published in 1953.

The medievalist Doderer must have delighted in writing this fairy tale about a Spanish knight, Ruy de Fanez, who sets out to win a duchess (complete with duchy) by riding through a large forest inhabited by a huge dragon. He does indeed encounter the dragon—knight and dragon depart vitually unharmed—and reaches the duchy, but feels that his life's purpose would not be fulfilled by marriage, so he returns to his life as a knight errant. Within a very short time he is killed while chasing plunderers from a village.

Doderer himself labelled his story a case of undeniable "escapism,"[16] adding provocatively "And why not?"; he claims to teach neither history nor attitudes (*Gesinnung*). Yet for all his denials and the flippantly applied label of escapism, *Das letzte Abenteuer* contains many of the characteristic elements of Doderer's stories: fateful encounters and sudden turning points, both leading to the individuation of the protagonist.

Ruy de Fanez is in his fortieth year—as was Doderer in 1936—and in spite of having spent his life as a wandering knight who has few friends and no family, he has a wealth of memories: "One was alone and carried a spread-out world in himself" (E, 389). Events in this story frequently trigger flights of memory in Ruy de Fanez, usually at inopportune moments like the climax of the encounter with the dragon, and a conversation with the duchess whom he came to woo. Doderer's memory experience is not synonymous with simply recalling past events or life's data. Rather it is the sudden appearance of a luminescent image, perhaps connected with a certain place, which emerges from the almost forgotten past, without carrying any necessary or obvious meaning. Moments of sudden daydreaming may reach the intensity of a mystical experience.

In the case of Ruy de Fanez, "there were lush valleys with quietly flowing streams, in which the greenery of the banks darkened in reflection. . ." (E, 389). Verdant surroundings and water imagery surround this knight errant, as well as many other Doderer heroes, most notably Melzer of *Die Strudlhofstiege*. The symbolism behind the water imagery, explored briefly by Franz P. Haberl,[17] carries largely positive meaning, but can signify destructive forces, as in *Die Wasserfälle von Slunj* (The Waterfalls of Slunj).

Ruy de Fanez is thus distinguished from the characters who surround him by his tendency to see himself at a certain point in a continuum of time. His glance is therefore not only retrospective but also directed into the future. An additional characteristic of Ruy de Fanez is his preoccupation with not interfering with the continuum

Turning Point

and accepting the uncertainty of no commitment. He also feels a certain detached curiosity as to what life may bring.

In *Das letzte Abenteuer* marriage to the toying and somewhat haughty duchess would be equivalent to living death for Ruy de Fanez. Doderer refers to the primitive superstition of walling a living being in the foundations of a new building to ensure the structure's firmness. For Ruy de Fanez, and to a lesser extent, for his friend Gamuret of Fronau, marriage represents such a walled-in, static existence. Both would rather embrace the uncertainty, including death, of a free future.

For Ruy de Fanez the turning point, which is marked by a flash of memory, comes during his encounter with the dragon. It is worthwhile to examine this scene in slightly greater detail because it portrays the crucial change in the hero, the *punctum nascendi*, the death of "character" and the birth of "person." Ruy's first reaction, while running toward the dragon, is one of disdain (*Hohn, Geringschätzung, ja Verachtung,*[18]) toward the duchess. The enormity of the dragon seems to be too overwhelming to serve as a proper test for would-be suitors. The lady—so it seems to Ruy—values herself too highly.

Presently, however, Ruy is face to face with the dragon that for some reason has closed its eyes, but he realizes that his sword is useless against this huge creature. At that point he experiences a feeling of inner emptiness (*in seinem Innern eine weite und lichte Leere*, D1A, 26), a sensation for which Doderer uses the metaphor of a house into which someone has recently moved and where hitherto unrecognized rooms are discovered. His inward look reveals to him that where fear of death should be there was nothing but a feeling of rest.

The journey of memory into his past is triggered by the dragon's opening its eyes. As we have seen in the case of the "tunnel eyes" of Jutta Bamberger, Doderer takes great care with the description of these organs of apperception. The eyes of the animal are compared to two small forest ponds into which the sun is shining, permitting us to see their "brown and moory bottom" (*brauner und mooriger Grund*). His glance into the dragon's eyes evokes memories of specific scenes within Ruy. But the scenes that Ruy relives are not necessarily significant events in his life. One image he recalls is a gentle valley with an abandoned mill and slowly flowing water. Compressed into a few moments, his past seems to him acceptable, and Doderer again finds an objective correlative for Ruy's sensation when he describes his memory as a "small bundle" which the knight suddenly finds to be light: "and—lo—he found it to be light" (D1A, 29).

From this point the actions of Ruy follow with the sureness of a sleepwalker. The prospect of continuing to woo and win the duchess seems suddenly quite incongruous. In fact, as soon as he is reunited with his squire and his servants, Ruy wants to return home. Continuing to the castle hardly even occurs to him, and it is only at the insistence of his squire that they do so. Because he recognizes with unshakable certainty that his destiny lies elsewhere, Ruy simply mumbles "all right" as he climbs on his horse.

The problem for Doderer, the storyteller, is now the continuation of the narrative. After a leisurely sojourn at the court, playing chess and daydreaming, Ruy leaves. He is attracted by the dragon; nevertheless, he proceeds indirectly and circuitously to the forest where the monster lives. He only manages to see the dragon from afar, but even that does not seem to matter. Ruy proceeds in a trance of heightened awareness. He notices details that hardly would have attracted his attention earlier, like the fluttering of the small flag on the point of his lance. Doderer compares this new seeing (*Schauen*—a favorite term of Goethe) to understanding a new language: "For the second time today the simple things of life approached him as if in a new language" (D1A, 103). After realizing and willingly following his own destiny, Ruy de Fanez is quite literally ready for anything including his own death.

Before Doderer concludes the story, he interjects a scene in which Ruy suddenly recalls his ability to improvise verses. While these would customarily be addressed to a lady, Ruy spontaneously recites them to the dragon, comparing the animal to fate itself. Looking into its eyes Ruy concludes that he is looking into the center of his own being (*in. die eigne Mitte*, D1A, 105). Doderer makes no attempt to moralize at this point or to attempt to define the center. At the moment when Ruy recites his verses aloud, a minstrel appears, the same one who had originally told him about the dragon and the duchess. Clearly an incarnation of Doderer (the slanted eyes of the minstrel are Doderer's customary signature), the minstrel invokes in his responsive song the multitude of possibilities of life and destiny. If there is any message in the story, it lies in Ruy's spontaneous readiness to accept his destiny without question or complaint.

To the *Reclam* edition of this story, Doderer has appended one of the most personal and subtle statements concerning the function of the "naturalistic" novel: ". . .to render all the terror or jumble [*Klimbim*] weightless, to suspend it, and finally, to change the eternally similar walls which surround us into windows through which we can look out while transcendence . . . shines in" (D1A, 125).

The short novel *Ein Umweg*, published in 1940, is directly connected with *Das letzte Abenteuer* not only because it is set in the past (in the seventeenth century), but also because one of the protagonists, Count Manuel Cuendias, assumes the name Ruy Fanez for his nocturnal escapades into student life. The novel also features a parallel to the encounter with the dragon, and considers fate and freedom, deliberateness and spontaneity, as well as the circuitous way (*Umweg*) to one's eventual fate.

Paul Brandter, a professional soldier during the Thirty Years' War, finds himself near execution for rather common transgressions against the civilian population. Brandter has always vaguely felt that he was destined for the gallows. Nevertheless, at the point of execution understandable fear causes him to cry out for someone to save his life. According to the custom of the day, a woman willing to marry the condemned man could save him from his death. A woman named Hanna responds to his plea, and Count Manuel, an officer of the Spanish Guard, helps in obtaining the necessary Imperial pardon. The remainder of the story represents a detour back to the beginning for Brandter, who this time will finally be executed.

The most interesting aspect of this novel is the fate of Count Manuel. While Brandter's life, from rescue to eventual execution, is simply a waiting period, rather than a development, Count Manuel's life changes dramatically. Having witnessed the spontaneity of Hanna's actions, Manuel gradually discovers or admits that he is in love with the woman who provides such a vivid contrast to the cold and calculating noblewomen who normally surround him. Manuel's change involves a departure from his usual sphere: the arrangements, plans, and rituals of Spanish court life. His love for Hanna remains unfulfilled, and he, like Brandter, finally experiences a rather ignominious death.

Hanna has been compared to a "demonic force"[19] which causes both Brandter and Manuel to stray from their destiny. For Brandter, the result of his rescue is a life of dull routine and subdued relationships with the people in his village, a stark contrast to the "free" life of the mercenary that he led before. But that former freedom which, he rightly thinks, must ultimately lead to his execution seems progressively more attractive to Brandter. As has been pointed out by S. H. Jones, his marriage to Hanna remains childless, a symbolic statement of the barrenness of their lives. Similarly, Manuel's regimented life becomes progressively more intolerable to him as a result of his love for Hanna. Manuel is one of the many Doderer characters who begins life on a "track," and being thrown off the track he is destined for doom.

In a parallel scene to Ruy de Fanez's encounter with the dragon, Manuel sets out on a chamois hunt. During the crucial moment when he should pull the trigger, he experiences a momentary trance and perceives inwardly a new direction for his life, "a new and happier track of his life."[20] His failure to kill the chamois seems completely incomprehensible to the others, who jokingly say that Manuel must have seen a monster (*ein Tatzelwurm*) to cause such paralysis. However, Manuel is, from now on, unwilling to submit to the norms of his society. He will not make excuses, but asserts his freedom by informing the curious hunters that he simply did not feel like shooting and that he had wished to be alone. Again, Doderer finds an apt symbol for Manuel's newfound freedom: the description of the bird of prey that is turning its leisurely and lonely circles high above the alpine landscape.

Manuel now finds himself unable to accept a marriage that has been arranged for him, and he even goes so far in his new life as to learn the undignified vernacular—the German language—with the aid of a student tutor, Rudolf Pleinacher. With him he also explores student life, using the alias Ruy Fanez. He delves into old books about monsters and is amazed by some tidbits from German Renaissance learning.

Eventually a second encounter with Hanna brings about the death of Manuel. During a military mission he happens to be stationed near the village where Brandter and Hanna live, and like an automaton, Manuel walks into his death. Just prior to that, he confides in a friend (named René) his thoughts on fate and freedom. He attempts to compare important resolutions one makes, concerning one's life, to the construction of a wall. The wall provides safety and form, "so that we can live at all, and not perish or become nothing, . . . like water one pours out" (U, 257). Within these constraints, he thinks, it should be possible to establish freedom. Doderer compares this self-made freedom to that obtained by a prisoner who paces his cell, but of his own free will chooses not to pace its entire length or width. Breaking through this wall of self-imposed restraint, of safe freedom, will lead to dissolution or death: "Because out there—I would say: Death is waiting in some form" (U, 258). Thus Manuel predicts his own apparently arbitrary doom.

The particular form of his death is slightly difficult to justify. Mistaking him for his wife's suspected lover, Brandter kills his former benefactor with one swift blow. Manuel's final moments before his death are full of embarrassment, stumbling against the door of Hanna's room, wandering around the house at night, and his death lacks any hint of triumph. By contrast, Brandter's execution contains hints of liberation and peace. Brandter, on the gallows, is quite literally raised above the gawking bystanders who are compared to a crowd of drowning people: "The people down there gave the impression of a huge crowd drowning whose faces, with their mouths, open were desperately straining upward" (U, 277).

Thus Brandter has traversed the detour of his life, which has brought him to the point where he was at the beginning of the novel. But now he accepts his fate. The detour is the theme and the central metaphor of this novel. Combining ideas of determinism and mysticism, Doderer seems to test the motif of the detour, which in *Die Strudlhofstiege* undergoes important variations. In the later novel, the detour represents not merely a delay in reaching the same predetermined goal, but takes on additional symbolic meaning signifying the essence of civilization: beauty and dignity.

The manuscript of *Ein Umweg* was to also become a keystone in Doderer's fortune as a novelist. His old friend and first publisher, Rudolf Haybach, sent the manuscript to the famous publishing house of C. H. Beck in Munich. The manuscript served as an introduction to a major publisher and was the beginning of a fruitful publisher-author relationship.

CHAPTER 3

The Breakthrough

I   Ein Mord den jeder begeht *(Every Man a Murderer)*

IN September of 1937 Doderer, residing in Dachau, the now infamous suburb of Munich, gave an oral preview of a novel on which he was working to Horst Wiemer, reader of C. H. Beck. Shortly thereafter Doderer signed a contract with Beck which freed him from major financial worries. In May 1938 *Ein Mord den jeder begeht (Every Man a Muderer,* tr. 1964), the first novel to introduce Doderer to a larger reading public, was published.

In Doderer's *Commentarii* of late August or early September 1937, we find a synopsis which may serve as the most reliable introduction to the content of the novel:

This is my novel: at the age of 15 a young man commits a murder without knowing that he did so. Under a veil of utterly coincidental details (most significant in informing us about his character) the most important event of his life passes him by. Neither at the moment of the deed nor later during his very normal life is my young man "intoxicated" [*berauscht*], divided within himself in a pathological sense, hypnotized, out of character, guilt-ridden. . . . Seven years later he marries, well and rich. A picture hangs in the house of his parents-in-law: the deceased older sister of his wife. This picture soon moves behind his wife, who seems to have stepped out of this frame, coarsened and without magic [*entzaubert*]. The dead woman seems to assume the stature of a "saint," becomes the true focus of his eros, which he seeks in vain in the living sister, his wife. . . . Our hero begins the search for the murderer because the officials had given up looking for the murderer more than five years ago. . . . He finds the trail, which leads to Berlin. The conclusions begin to be compelling. As if he were stepping closer to a mirror in a big, dim hall: he sees someone coming towards him, it is he himself, it must be he, the murderer of the unknown beloved: now he recognizes him. He has proofs in hand. It is himself.[1]

The focus of the novel is simultaneously the retracing of Conrad's

The Breakthrough

steps, the unravelling of the mystery, and the development of the protagonist. The process of slow discovery of the true nature of crucial events in his life is at the same time the process of his gradual humanization. As Dietrich Weber has pointed out, the usual forward movement of a novel of development (*Entwicklungsroman*) is reversed in *Mord* (DW, 47).

The puzzling aspect of Doderer's novel lies, in part, in his assertions on fate in general, and in the provocative aspect of the *jeder* ("everyone") contained in its title. We must examine whether the unintentional "murder" committed by Conrad Castiletz can be seen as symptomatic of the way his character is constituted, and whether or not we may conclude that Conrad's blindness towards the murder (the parallel to the Oedipus myth has been pointed out [DW, 47]) is more than an individual fate.

In no other novel up to this time, with the possible exception of the "Jutta Bamberger" fragment, did Doderer portray the youth and adolescence of a character with such care and insight. Doderer's rationale is clear from the first lines of the novel: "Everyone has his childhood dumped over his head like a bucket. Later we find out what was in it. But it runs down for an entire lifetime, you can change clothes or costumes as much as you want" (Mord, 5).[2] The decisive nature of childhood influences could hardly be stated more concisely and imaginatively, and the slightly ludicrous image is characteristic of Doderer because it prevents any possibility of hidden pomposity in an opening general assertion. Critics have not yet explored in sufficient depth the facts relating to the years before Conrad commits the "murder."

The first overwhelming influence in Conrad's life is that of his father, who was forty-seven years old when Conrad was born, and who, although generally a gentle man, has outbursts of intense, irrational, and violent anger. These episodes of shouting and physical abuse haunt Conrad in his dreams and contribute to a lifelong tendency not to draw attention to himself. Conrad loves his quiet, tolerant, but slightly ineffective and inefficient mother. In her presence he plays quietly for hours. Doderer ascribes to her the nearly untranslatable adjective *blümerant* (dizzy, giddy, and superficial).

Little Conrad's playing symbolically foreshadows certain aspects of his future. The little boy has an uncanny sense of time, planning the activities of his tin soldiers over eight-day sequences. The sense of temporality and of thinking ahead, as well as remembering, will gradually be severely stunted, and the adult Conrad will painstakingly have to reestablish it. Another game of his childhood—playing with his large toy railroad—anticipates the multiple literal and symbolic functions of the railroad tracks and tunnels which occur throughout the novel. The tracks symbolize a routinely predictable life, the predetermined nature of events, and the smoothly running "program."

Aside from his parents, the two major focal points for young Conrad are the school and an area full of meadows, woods, and ponds not far from his home. The ponds contain salamanders, tadpoles, and other amphibians which some of the young city boys sell for pennies to an aquarium. The significance of the salamander episodes is two-fold: They provide the author with the opportunity to contrast Conrad with the other, "smarter" boys, and provide the rich symbolism of the primitive animals for which Doderer had a particular interest. In fact, one of the largest of the salamanders becomes an emblem for the dignity of the individual and the legitimacy of Conrad's individuality.

From the beginning of these play episodes, Conrad's manner is contrasted to that of the other boys. He speaks correctly, and his naive honesty stands in vivid contrast to their slangy and sly ways, their "in-group" behavior. Conrad's punctiliousness and conscientiousness prevent his being accepted by the crowd. He wants to be part of the group, and he believes that particularly audacious acts will win him respect and acceptance. If there is a beginning manifestation of Conrad's flaw, it must be seen in his boyish tendency to boast, to outdo others, to win. We may surmise that the appropriate path would have been for him to accept his individuality. As it is, his adolescent boasting leads him to one of the most senseless and brutal acts of his childhood and an anticipation of the actual murder.

The boys playing at the pond prevent a beautiful and gentle ring snake from reaching the shore. Repeatedly they catch it and toss it back into the water. At one point during this game Conrad becomes conscious of a decisive moment in his life, an irretrievable opportunity to assert himself in defiance of the mob, but he lacks the inner strength. Instead, in his effort to outdo the others, he tosses the snake far out into the pond where it collides with a protruding branch and is killed.

The paragraph describing the struggle within Conrad deserves full attention:

Something now stirred in Kokosch, something that may be called the awareness of a decisive moment. Here at last was his chance to release the thing that had lain compressed within him whenever he associated with these boys, like a spring held down. Now was the moment to release it, at any cost. He could tear the cords that bound him, could step aside, even if it meant that he would be left standing alone, with the others angry or even hostile toward him. (M, 25)

In spite of outdoing his peers or perhaps because of it, he is forever alienated from the crowd. Considering the time and place of the writing of this novel, the temptation to allegorize these thoughts is strong but erroneous.

One boy serves as a model that Conrad is unable to imitate. When he first meets Günther Ligharts, Conrad listens with astonishment to his stories about dinosaurs, not because of the intrinsic interest of the subject, but because Günther has taken the initiative to learn something on his own. He has thus of his own volition given direction to his life. To that extent Günther Ligharts is free. Conrad observes: "So you could turn your attention to something of your own free will and by your own decision. So you could go in any direction you pleased" (M, 22).

Another aspect of Conrad's character is highlighted by Günther's presence. When the episode with the killing of the snake has forever spoiled playing at the pond, Conrad decides to release all of the salamanders he has been keeping in his terrarium. Günther's simple question: "Have you observed them enough?" surprises Conrad, who concludes that he really doesn't know what Günther means by "observe" (*beobachten*). Thus his deficient vision, his inability to perceive openly ("apperceive"), is made evident. Like his father, Conrad seems occasionally blinded. He fails to assess the effect of his actions on others, and is unwilling, too lazy, or unable to look clearly at the present or the future. At times he seems paralyzed and unable to act straightforwardly, and at other times he acts thoughtlessly and hastily, often with a disastrous outcome.

In contrast, Günther deals with problems in a straightforward way. He is able to observe and state his intentions clearly. A northerner in a southern environment, he is comparable to Conrad in that he speaks clearly and correctly. But in contrast to Conrad, he has no desire to become a member of any group. He is secure in his individuality. The only encounter of Günther and Conrad with the group of salamander-hunting boys highlights the difference between the two boys. As they are on their way to release Conrad's salamanders, some boys attempt to block their way. One of them mocks Günther's manner of talking and is swiftly hit in the face by

Günther. Spontaneously Günther has found the way to get the respect of punks which Conrad has failed to get by condescending to them.

With the release of the salamanders and Günther's departure for Berlin, a segment of Conrad's life is completed. He becomes interested in chemistry sets and finds satisfaction in conducting simple experiments. At the point where Conrad experiences peace and seems to have discovered a new world for himself, he witnesses a terrifying episode from his window: A man, pursued by the police, shoots himself in the head. Shortly before pulling the trigger, he glances around, and Conrad is able to see the white of his eyes. A few days later his father has one of his most violent outbursts of anger, beating and kicking his son mercilessly. The anguish Conrad witnesses, or experiences, results in a sense of being "in a hot and dry isolation from himself and the world. . ." (M, 42/3). Doderer thus expresses the symbolic dryness and lifelessness of Conrad's inner being, of his father's character, and—to some extent—his own. Two days after the beating, Conrad wakes up from a dream, crying: "He wept because of Ligharts, because of his father, because of the dead man who had lain by the lumber below, because of the salamanders, because of what had happened and what was now, because of yesterday, today, and tomorrow, and so perhaps for a whole life" (M, 44). This is the last time Conrad cries spontaneously.

Conrad develops a need to protect himself from incursions of terror from the outside. His insecurity manifests itself, in part, in his habit of standing in his room for a few moments, before going anywhere, thinking through the plans for what is to come, to "listen" inwardly and to check that everything is all right, to make dispositions, so that nothing surprising or threatening can approach him. Frequently, however, he cannot rid himself of the vague feeling that something is not right (*nicht in Ordnung*).

One curious and symbolic game Conrad plays involves a large old, nearly "blind" mirror. Squinting, Conrad approaches it, and at a certain point, it seems to him that the reflection looks at him with black holes where there should be eyes. Stepping back from the mirror and approaching it, he slowly makes out the suggestion of a skull, thereby anticipating the discovery of the murderer, as we have already seen in Doderer's synopsis.

The murder takes place when Conrad is fifteen years old. He finds himself in a train compartment with a group of boisterous, drinking students. Conrad, who like so many of Doderer's characters, has a heightened olfactory sense, is slightly repulsed by various smells in the compartment. He briefly considers that he might take a seat elsewhere, but, as in the earlier episode, he lacks decisiveness. One of the medical students has a skull with him, and the boys suddenly seize on the plan that they should put it on a stick and wave it outside the window of the adjacent compartment occupied by a young lady traveling alone. When it has to be decided who will hold the skull, Conrad immediately volunteers. As a result of this prank, the lady is killed as she leans out of the window of the train which is at that moment speeding through a tunnel. Until his marriage to the dead woman's sister, the memory of this journey is dim, in part because of the angry reaction of his father when he is told about the event.

Among the many carefully composed parallels and juxtapositions in the novel, one episode contrasting with the killing of the snake stresses the positive potential of Conrad. While on vacation at an aunt's house in the country, Conrad plays at a pond and suddenly discovers a large crayfish at the bottom of the clear water. His reactions are quite different from the earlier episode. He wants to catch the crayfish and eventually does so, but he is extremely careful to do no harm to the animal. He simply *observes* the crayfish returning to his domain. Conrad briefly considers taking the crayfish with him, but—thinking of his aunt's cooking pots—decides to leave him free. Sitting at the edge of the pond, alone, Conrad finds happiness. The crayfish is variously referred to as "thoughtful inhabitant" (*bedächtiger Bewohner*), "monster from the deep" (*Ungeheuer der Tiefe*). and "mysterious guest" (*geheimnisvoller Gast*). In *Die Strudlhofstiege*, the main character, Melzer, is repeatedly adorned with the epithet "crayfish" (*Krebs*). Considering a crayfish's backward motion in the water, we may see it as the mystery of the past, of unknown, forgotten, or repressed aspects of one's personal history.

The first part of the novel, and with it Conrad's adolescence, includes a number of love affairs. Under the pernicious influence of his cynical, Mephistophelian tutor Albert Lehnder, Conrad abruptly cuts off a relationship with Ida Plangl because, in the opinion of his tutor, he is becoming "too involved." The contrast between Conrad and his paramour is telling. Whereas Ida does not probe into his past, she does make Conrad remember certain events of his childhood, even though it is painful for him. Conrad is even tempted to lie and tries to suppress his memory. Doderer uses water imagery and other symbols of flowing, life, and cleanliness to present the love affair in a positive way.

Lehnder persuades Conrad to break off the relationship, arguing that life must have order, which here is synonymous with aloofness, lack of involvement, and sterility. He warns him of the possibility of fathering a child. Not wanting to be disturbed any longer and to come face to face with the unpredictable, including the love of Ida Plangl, Conrad, for the sake of order, eliminates emotion from his life. As Conrad drops the farewell letter to Ida into the mailbox, the narrator comments ironically: "The spirits of order did not speak up. They did not give the expected sign of lively assent, and his self-confidence did not rise like a balloon when sandbags have been jettisoned" (M, 86). Conrad merely feels awkward.

The death of his mother and the death of Ida Plangl bring to a close the first part of the novel. Conrad has no tears for his mother, but experiencing finality does have an impact on him. His father is portrayed at the graveside as anguished, but, at the same time, ridiculous in the display of his emotions; he stands at the grave, biting his hat, ". . . with a face that was small and wet like that of a crying infant" (M, 98). The death of Ida Plangl is surrounded by biblical images of sterility. It so happens that Ida dies in Salzburg, and when Conrad hears of her death he imagines, in the following manner, the castle that dominates the city and the surrounding countryside: "But now, deep within himself, he saw Salzburg on a perfectly level plain, a towering castle of white, dry color set in an endless, salty steppe" (M, 100). The imagery of sterility reflects Conrad's emotional state, and Doderer underlines the contrast by surrounding him with images of flowing water and early spring.

Successful in business, married to the sister of the woman who died in the train many years ago, Conrad Castiletz is smoothly following the tracks established for him early on by his father. But all is not well. The picture of his wife's sister, Louison Veik, haunts him. Under the influence of Herr von Hohenlocher, Conrad begins to daydream, assisted by liberal quaffs of gin. His life, though, continues undisturbed. His wife develops an intense interest in sports and spends much of her time in the company of her ski instructor. Only occasional intrusions of irrationality disturb the smooth flow of life. Mysteriously, the portrait of Louison Veik induces notions such as the following in Conrad: "Confronting this portrait, and in a fraction of a second, Conrad became vividly aware of something he had never before conceived: the possibility of a life altogether different

The Breakthrough

from his own. Even switching into another track became imaginable—became, in a strange way, a reality" (M, 155).

Conrad gradually begins to acquire a past (M, 178). He becomes familiar with detailed accounts of the police investigations which have failed to turn up the murderer of Louison Veik. Fearful dreams of gigantic Salamanders (named Benjamin) haunt him, and a terrifying episode occurs, which parallels the suicide witnessed by Conrad when he was young. During a peaceful moment when Conrad and his wife are together, a blood-curdling scream is heard. It is the cry of a mother whose child has run into the street and is almost hit by a car.

Gradually Conrad mellows, becomes more receptive, and turns inward. Doderer's reference to a bowl in a fountain which openly receives the flowing water is symbolic for his new state of mind (M, 243). Conrad finds time and opportunity to retrace his steps, discovering the true circumstances of Louison Veik's death.

His journey to Berlin, at the beginning of part IV of the novel, opens with a powerful Expressionistic portrait of the city, its mindless bustle and its gigantic underground transportation system. In Berlin he meets some of the former passengers in the train compartment on the night of the fateful prank. One of them has seen the death of Louison Veik and can clarify the entire episode.

The discovery leads to the final and decisive *Verwandlung* of Conrad. He is initially tempted to bemoan his fate and to make excuses. He feels that he has not lived at all, but rather that he has been handed on like a parcel. At the same time he experiences a new lightness, recovers his memory of significant scenes from his youth, and unlike his father, experiences a moment of conversion. As is usual with Doderer, the conversion includes the discovery (initially manifested by his refusal to mouth clichés) of a new language: "But then he saw the irrationality of what he intended to say, and the folly of the way he had spoken all his life, the way everyone spoke, taking from mouth to mouth smooth and borrowed phrases. It was like a flash of grace, illuminating everything with a surpassing clarity" (M, 361). After the discovery and *Verwandlung* Conrad is whisked off to his accidental, albeit carefully foreshadowed, death.

The question that must finally be asked and answered concerns the general validity of Conrad's fate, as indicated by the *jeder* in the title. To the extent that we act in accordance with what we think others expect of us, instead of following our own conscience, we are indeed guilty of the symbolic "murder" of our individuality. To the extent that there are events in our childhood or adolescence which produce shame, guilt, or pain we suppress because they would make us feel uncomfortable, we are again guilty of "murder." Inherent in the theme of the novel is a somewhat romantic notion of individual destiny. But, in spite of skillful composition, vivid dialogues, numerous powerful passages (such as the description of the city at the beginning of part IV), the novel fails to convince us of the general validity of Conrad's fate, in part because of the esoteric aspects of his life, and the contrived sequence of accidents. No attempt has yet been made to interpret Conrad Castiletz as a German "Everyman" of the 1930s. Perhaps an interesting case could be made.

II Die erleuchteten Fenster oder Die Menschwerdung des Amtsrates Julius Zihal
(The Illuminated Windows or The Humanization of Councillor Julius Zihal)

In 1939 Doderer completed a novel which was not published until 1950. Events in *Die erleuchteten Fenster oder Die Menschwerdung des Amtsrates Julius Zihal* run conveniently parallel to the rigid order of Nazi ideology and its attempts at totalitarian control. Once again, Doderer's protagonist is changed and spends the evening of his life in a somewhat idyllic state. In *Zihal*, written after he had already begun working on *Die Dämonen*, Doderer speaks with the slightly condescending, yet loving, manner that was part of his repertoire. With its exuberant, hyperbolic, grotesque humor, frequent asides, easy intimacy with the "distinguished reader," citations from tax rules, and old-fashioned type setting, the novel is reminiscent of the tone of Sterne or Jean Paul.

Zihal has been an exemplary civil servant in the Austro-Hungarian bureaucracy, which is allegorized throughout the novel by the image of the double eagle.[3] He has internalized the methodical and impersonal manner of this bureaucracy, which has attempted to achieve an omnipresence of order and rules unparalleled even in the German-speaking realms. Zihal prides himself in not reading novels, but in knowing almost by heart the "codex" of the "Taxamt" which he served. The "mystical or at least mysterious institution"[4] may stand for any totalitarian realm which considers its end to be itself, and which, in its hubris, elaborately constructs what Doderer calls the "second reality" (*zweite Wirklichkeit*). One of the results of Zihal's internalization of order is his inability to relate to human beings except through imagining their *Aktwerdung* ("becoming a file"), when they stand for some issue, can be fitted into some preestablished category, thus attaining the honorific status of a file. The very word *Aktwerdung* serves as a humorous contrast to *Menschwerdung* ("becoming a human being").

After his retirement, Zihal moves into a new apartment, which, the first time, he enters in darkness. He is suddenly fascinated by the possibility of watching other people in their "illuminated windows" while he remains in safe darkness. With his customary thoroughness, he embarks upon his "hobby" of harmless voyeurism. His compulsion to miss nothing, to record, number, label, and classify, all human and all-too-human phenomena is strong. He associates small unaccustomed liberties with extreme license. Smoking a cigar or visiting a café at a pleasurably unusual hour represents "a world having become free and changeable" (Z, 39), which is in conflict with the rigid order of Zihal's personality.

Within Zihal's world, small freedoms represent chaos, but it is clearly the author's intent to demonstrate that chaos functions in a positive manner because the narrator refers to "constructive chaos" (*das constructive Chaos*, Z, 74). Order, or its more harmless cousin, orderliness, has separated Zihal from many innocent pleasures, has closed him off as if he were living in a bag—we already know Doderer's penchant for ludicrous images: "He felt so to speak as if being stuck in a sack tied at the top, standing next to life" (Z, 72).[5] This sack is said to act like a filter which permits only abstractions to pass through. But now and then a "weakness," a constructive flaw, becomes evident: For example, Zihal is quite susceptible to the beauty of women. In his own way—in spite of his formality and decorum—he is a very loving person.

Zihal, like Conrad Castiletz and many other Doderer protagonists, approaches his *Verwandlung* by way of contemplative states and daydreaming: "It was beautiful standing here in the dark and to glance deeply inward and far away, it was beautiful, even without—objects. . . (Z, 74). This "object-less" contemplation may be focused on a ray of sunlight which is shing on a box of shoe polish, or, more sensuously and object-filled, on Zihal's recurring dream of a wine-growing region near Vienna, suffused with Dionysian warmth.

The protracted symbolic struggle between total order and constructive chaos is the most striking and important aspect of the novel. Lifelessness, quiet, darkness—metaphorically varied throughout—are engaged in battle with chaos, warmth, human contact, and light. Zihal approaches his humanization from its opposite.

His *Vertierung* is underscored by the terms "troglodyte" and "worm," which are applied to him when he must crawl on the floor to avoid being watched by someone who is doing precisely what Zihal is doing—observing others through a telescope. The humorous climax of Zihal's observations comes during a scene when he focuses his binoculars on a window from which another pair of lenses stares back at him. Doderer compares the scene to a naval battle, but without sound: "Nothing moved, it was deadly still and ice-light [*eishell*]. The artillery fired incessantly and without a sound. But Zihal's flag ship of total order took in water first and went down" (Z, 96 - 97). The point zero and the destruction of the old Zihal occur when he falls off the table on which he is precariously perched with his telescope. Zihal is not seriously hurt, but his telescope breaks into pieces. Doderer's description of the "fallen" Zihal emphasizes the theme of chaos and humanization: "What was he now to look at, our councillor? Was it still he? No, that is no longer a councillor; we can't call the thing that is rumbling around among debris and darkness a 'councillor.' It is: chaos. . . . For seconds our Julius submerged deeply into the primeval chaotic state, as if he wanted to get a last running start for his now final humanization. . ." (Z, 181).

From a brief illness Zihal recovers as a changed person. He now reacts in a comparatively uncomplicated way. His stilted speech, which used to be laced with official jargon, has given way to the lilt and suppleness of Viennese dialect. He can now shrug off old habits, so that when Rosl Oplatek, whom he has loved from a distance for some time, comes to visit him, he casually offers her the binoculars, once the instruments of his futile obsession with total control. (He had used the binoculars for his observations of nude women, recording every instance, every angle, every sight, with painstaking accuracy). Complicated stories have been spun around these old field glasses to illustrate the importance which Zihal invested in them. But now he offers them to Rosl with the words: "Rosl. . .you keep the 'looker' [*den Gucker*], for my sake, and to remember today" (Z, 191). Doderer underscores the new relationship of Zihal and Rosl in another subtle way: Rosl is going to the "Hof-Oper" for the first time in her life, and on that evening Mozart's *The Magic Flute*, one of the finest celebrations of love and humaneness, is being performed.

Zihal thus follows the pattern of *Verwandlung* familiar from many works of Doderer. This novel, however, is distinguished by the ironic and constantly refracting commentary of the narrator. This is also the first novel in which Doderer pulls a considerable number of stops

The Breakthrough

on the instrument of his humor. Using quotes from the tax manual, Latin citations, and constant asides to the reader, his style is as ironic and contorted as that of Jean Paul. It provides us with an ironic look into the petty world of Kakania, into "a kakanian. . .citizen's inner being" (Z, 7).[6] However, in Zihal the potential viciousness of overwhelming bureaucracy remains merely a possibility, not a source of eternal frustration and unrelenting gloom such as we find in the works of Franz Kafka.

For its exuberance, virtuosity, and conciseness *Zihal* can be compared only to Doderer's own *Die Merowinger oder Die totale Familie*. Unfortunately, its arcane allusions are virtually untranslatable. The precise subdivisions of the Austrian bureaucratic hierarchy have few parallels in the Anglo-American experience.

CHAPTER 4

Apogee

I Tangenten *(Tangents)*

DODERER'S voluminous *Tangenten, Tagebuch eines Schriftstellers 1940 - 1950* (Tangents. Diary of a Writer, published 1964) is the main document informing us of the author's life and thought during the war and immediate postwar years. From 1940 to 1945 Doderer wore the uniform of a German Air Force captain, and one of his assignments was screening applications for various officers' training programs. The story "Unter schwarzen Sternen" (Under Black Stars, tr. 1974, *Chicago Review*) portrays the day-to-day tasks of examining and selecting variously motivated young men, and describes the morbid atmosphere of Vienna after the *Anschluss*.

Tangenten betrays a surprising detachment, balanced with a continuing concern for philosophical, intellectual, and literary issues, with little explicit comment on the day-to-day politics or excesses of the time. Doderer felt curiously victimized and helpless. He stresses that he considered the reigning totalitarian ideology of Nazism equivalent to a "second reality", an artificial construct heedless of the individual, a system imposing collective behavior, thought, and expectation on everyone. It is difficult to determine whether or not he makes a convincing case for his attitude of simply awaiting the return to "first reality," or nonideological normalcy. As a somewhat eccentric writer, whose work is clearly antitotalitarian, who does not celebrate a German way of life or a German destiny, and who had been married to a Jewish woman, Doderer seems to have felt that he could best escape prosecution in the officers corps, the traditional occupation of the nobility.

An entry that recurs in his diaries from the war years reads: "He who understands and knows the way can live comfortably even in hell." This Eastern wisdom is underlined by a Taoistic saying which

Doderer also quotes with a great deal of seriousness: "The wise man does not act and the populace lives happily" (T, 321). This notion of not acting, not affecting, not interfering, is intellectually grounded in Doderer's belief in the duty of the novelist to accept the world as it is. In one of his later essays Doderer even defines the narrative poet as "someone who wants neither to work on the world nor on himself; truly a person without aims."[1] In his opinion, it would have been utterly useless to counter a pernicious ideology with yet other ideological statements. Fanaticism in one direction cannot be "cured" by fanaticism in another. Pseudological, demonic activity renders thinking people helpless and, of necessity, inactive. It is useful to remember that in 1939 Doderer converted to Catholicism. The following statement on the fate of the Nazi rule mirrors an almost religious submission: "The miserable state of affairs has to be borne patiently and knowingly, *as such*, it is part of life, it cannot be put outside of life as something that 'doesn't count.' Everything counts, first of all, every second, and secondly—if you look at it carefully—you have neither the ability nor the competence to distinguish" (T, 12).

Political solutions from the left and right wings seemed equally dubious to Doderer, who simply did not accept the idea that he should propose any "solutions." His terse comment on politicians asserts that it is the politician's deepest wish that there should be no life (T, 22). And he rejects the revolutionary on the grounds that he destroys history insofar as all history becomes "pre-history to his own revolution" (T, 30). Attempts at realizing an earthly paradise are both blasphemous and idiotic.

What *Zihal* portrayed in fictional guise, Doderer spells out in *Tangenten:*

Every principle of order, which is on the same level with that which is to be ordered, must lead to an infinite number of ordering efforts and hence to cruelty; in every pedant who arranges pencils or tools in a parallel fashion, who announces and sanctifies an eternally fixed place for the matches, who tortures laundry by constant re-counting, and at the same time tortures all who live with him, his wife, his children—in each such pedant there lives a Genghis Khan, who, if you would loosen him upon the world, would try nothing less than to fixate the moveable differential between *quantitas* and *qualitas* and to bring psychological time to a standstill. (T, 34)

Doderer's jump from laundry-counting to the terminology of

scholasticism is his typical device for achieving clarity through understatement.

In the final analysis, Doderer's poetics are based on acceptance of reality *as it is,* and his insistence on "Apperception" as one of the highest virtues harks back not only to Aristotle's concept of "mimesis" but to the poetics of the Romantic movement, particularly to the Schlegel brothers, who maintained that the composition of legitimate works of art parallels in a nonrational way the composition of the universe, and thus that the work of the poet parallels the work of God. The appearance of disorder and Romantic irony gradually permits apperception of underlying order, just as the phenomena in the natural world offer us the appearance of disorder, through which we may perceive the wisdom of God.[2] In *Tangenten* Doderer clarifies this matter: "To agree at all times, *hic et nunc,* and right away, means to love God's unfathomable plans above everything and to love the intentions of His work which are so hard for us short-timers to await, and to love the forever open composition of His work" (T, 45). Particularly in the later works, Doderer's concern with open-ended yet not fragmentary composition signifies his readiness to change and to adjust to new realities.

Aside from specific commentaries on *Die Dämonen* and *Die Strudlhofstiege, Die Tangenten* features a helter-skelter array of insights and occasional references to the soldier's life. There are also interesting biographical observations, which in the end trail off into a so-called *Liber Epigrammaticus* containing pithy definitions of various themes similar to the collection of sayings in Doderer's *Repertorium. Tangenten* permits us to follow Doderer's crisscross journey through warring Europe, finally ending in Norway, where, amid the debacle of the last days of the war, Doderer was working on one of his finest, most Mozartean novels, *Die Strudlhofstiege.* After the war was over, Doderer noted rather laconically his relief that "first reality" had returned.

Tangenten remains of greatest importance to anyone interested in the origin and the work in progress of *Die Strudlhofstiege* and *Die Dämonen.* The latter had been begun in the years 1930 - 31, and was complete up to the first part (seventeen chapters). But for various reasons Doderer interrupted work on the novel. A good case can be made for the explanation that the events portrayed in *Die Dämonen,* occurring in 1927, were still too close for objective treatment. To what extent Doderer's flirtation with Nazism and his subsequent disillusionment figured in the beginning and the interruption of *Die Dämonen* is and will remain a subject for speculation.

II Die Strudlhofstiege oder Melzer und die Tiefe der Jahre
   (*The Strudlhof Steps, or Melzer and the Depth of the Years*)

Doderer placed a stumbling block in the way of summarizing his novels by asserting dogmatically: "A work of narrative art is all the more legitimate the less a summary of contents will give us an idea of it."[3] Any attempt to paraphrase the contents of *Die Strudlhofstiege* would reveal a lack of outward action. To be sure, there are intrigues of one kind or another, and there is the meticulous description of Mary K.'s accident, but the unique lyrical value of *Die Strudlhofstiege* cannot be conveyed by a plot summary.

In spite of the difficulty in approaching its contents, Herbert Eisenreich has outlined the significance of this novel within the context of European literature:

The novel *Die Strudlhofstiege* may be judged from whatever aspect: it keeps what had been variously promised for half a century. What was tried here and there . . . is combined by Doderer, it seems effortlessly, in this complex of 900 pages:

A subject matter appropriate to the novel, i.e. the closed, but multi-levelled Viennese society during the years shortly before and after the first world war, whereby the novel even fulfills a historiographic function (in contrast to Musil's caricature of Kakania);

a significant theme, i.e. the story of someone who went out to become a normal human being (something that novelists didn't consider necessary for 50 years);

an empirical universe that can be tested in its details, intimate psychological knowledge and a trained intelligence; a manner of representation that is in accord with life, i.e. non-ideological;

a language which grasps supple and tender emotions as well as concrete realities, whose mother is the Viennese dialect and whose father is Latin;

a vocabulary, increased *ad hoc* by Doderer's own creations, becoming nearly encyclopedic, providing the nutrients for wit and humor;

and—without considering our enumeration comprehensive—an eye toward composition constantly checked at the drawing board, even though that does not explain the composition, so that we are reminded of a work of architecture (of the Strudlhof staircase in Vienna's IXth district), as well as of a symphony.[4]

There are nevertheless several obstacles the sympathetic reader has to overcome in approaching *Die Strudlhofstiege*. The difficulty lies in the complicated structure of the novel.[5] Simple chronological sequence did not suffice in order to consider the fates of approximately twenty characters because their lives run parallel to each other. To achieve a measure of simultaneity, it became necessary constantly to retrace, to begin again at earlier moments, each time with a different focal point. But the difficulty in reading the novel does not arise from the structure alone, but also from the sudden shifts from one time and place to another. The clearest example of Doderer's efforts at achieving simultaneity comes toward the end of the novel, moments before Mary K.'s accident. Minute by minute, Doderer follows the paths of a number of characters who come together at the scene of the accident. To be sure, he assists the reader with frequent asides, jolting our memory and helping us see relationships.

Doderer defended his manner of telling a story with subsequent theoretical considerations. In his essay on "Grundlagen und Funktion des Romans" (Bases and Function of the Novel), he cites the prodigious nineteenth-century novelist Friedrich Spielhagen, who had made some basic observations concerning the writing of novels. Doderer paraphrases Spielhagen as follows: (1) The epic imagination has as its object nothing other than the world itself, and thus the epic writer (the novelist) strives to offer a view of the world. (2) The nature of the epic imagination clashes with the nature of art, which must impose limits. (3) This fundamental paradox can never be completely resolved. (4) The means for an approximate resolution of the paradox is found in the attempt to make the most complete use of objective representation. The aesthetic value of the novel rises as this method is more or less successfully applied (WdD, 154). These observations are contiguous to Doderer's theory of the "total novel."

Lest it be thought that Doderer simply reiterates fundamental assertions of Naturalism, it must be pointed out that in the same essay he cites E. M. Forster's ideas concerning the parallel between the novel and the symphony. Thus the primacy of the musical model—the fundamental shift in twentieth-century aesthetics—applies to Doderer as well. Not only the mimetic aspects alluded to by Spielhagen, but also the essentially irrational or associative aspects of musical composition apply to modern literature and to Doderer's novels.

Aside from the four-movement composition of the novel, Doderer more specifically follows a musical technique introduced by Beethoven, beginning with a chapter or section far away from the main key and then gradually modulating to the main action. This technique of suspension is illustrated in *Die Strudlhofstiege* in the scene where Geyrenhoff and his friends meet in his room for a nightcap. From the room one can hear the rushing of a stream that is driving a mill wheel. Doderer introduces this section by describing with Homeric leisure the movable gutter used to guide the water to the mill wheel. Finally, after a technically detailed description of the progress of the water, the noise made by the mill reaches the window of Geyrenhoff's room. The gradual shift from the seemingly unimportant periphery to the center of the action is a frequent narrative technique of Doderer.

To the four-movement structure, the use of a central unifying symbol, leitmotifs, and "off-key" introductions, we may add sudden false conclusions as parallels to musical composition. In one scene leading to a gathering of several of the main characters at the Strudlhof steps, Ingrid Schmeller is to meet her friend Semski for a last farewell. Ingrid's father, who disapproves of their friendship, is secretly following his daughter in order to thwart their meeting. Doderer also describes how several others participating in the scene are approaching the steps. When Ingrid reaches the top of the steps the action casually switches to another character. Although suspense is created through this technique, Doderer's offhanded manner suggests that he is not merely searching for detective-story effects, but uses rapid shifts as an attempt to achieve simultaneity.

In the "Grundlagen und Funktion des Romans" Doderer also focuses on a second idea which may help one to approach *Die Strudlhofstiege:* the crucial importance of memory in writing and structuring a novel. Beginning with a nonrational core remembrance, the narrator becomes a vehicle for his own memory. Events and places must first have been forgotten (WdD, 158) and through the selectivity of memory rise to the narrative surface. The choice between important and unimportant aspects or events is thus seemingly automatic. The narrator becomes a medium, and his authenticity rests on his sensibility in recalling or forgetting past events. A compromise is reached, and the paradox is partially resolved between the attempt at total coverage and the demands of artistic selectivity. Hence the fundamental importance of the person and function of the narrator in Doderer's novels.

The nonrational *punctum nascendi* of *Die Strudlhofstiege* is found in the year 1916, when Doderer was in Siberia, where the image of the elaborately cascading steps rose before him. Twenty-eight years later, in May 1942, while he was stationed at Ryshkovo near

Kursk, the same memory of the Strudlhof Steps rose again, and this time the diary entries slowly grew into the novel. The most authentic statement on the symbolic significance of the steps in Doderer's own words is found in *Die Strudlhofstiege* which are reiterated in his essay on "Bases and Function of the Novel":

> From such veils [the steps] emerged. There they were, twenty-eight years after they had first appeared to me in Eastern Asia: they seemed to grow, or rather to descend, and in doing so they divided the sudden and unimaginative decline of the terrain. In this way the land, inarticulate and almost meaninglessly abrupt, was subdivided into numerous graceful turns so that one's glance did not simply slide down the incline, but fell slowly like a swinging and hesitating autumn leaf. And this is how it became visibly clear that every way and every path (even in our own garden) is more than a connection between two points, one of which you leave to reach the other. Rather, each path has its own essence that is more than simply a direction which may guide you, or a pretense which may disappear while you walk. . . . Here [on the Strudlhof steps] one would have to stride upward or march downward, one could not possibly scurry up and down as if [the steps] were a chicken coop ladder. . . . The steps lay there for everyone, for the smug rabble and the riff-raff, but they were designed to prepare one for the strides of fate. . . [the steps] are always there, and they never tire of telling us that each way has its own dignity, and that in all cases the path is more than the goal. The master-builder of the steps took a small piece of the millions of paths in the city and showed us how much dignity and decorum is intrinsic in every yard. . . . If the walk becomes expression on these steps, and if someone who has lost his dignity now seems forced to explain his descent more explicitly than before, then, in spite of the decline, the deepest intent of the builder has been fulfilled: he has explicated for his countrymen the preciousness of every part of the steps. . . . (WdD, 271 - 72)

We recognize the correspondence between objects (or landscapes) and states of inner being, which Doderer had nurtured ever since his first collection of verse. But now this correspondence is fully and confidently articulated, and the steps serve as the concrete and, at the same time, indirect and complex symbol. The steps divide and compose, lend form to what was amorphous, simple and unadorned. By following their serpentine descent, those who walk on them are forced into an indirect, decorous, and perhaps contemplative approach. The comparison of the steps and the chicken-coop ladder provides vivid contrast. Dietrich Weber has pointed out that those characters in the novel who experience the deepest meaning of the steps are those who walk on them, who follow their path, their indirect descent.

The Strudlhof steps also stand for the circuitous manner in which we seem to arrive at goals or fulfill our destinies, and are therefore contiguous to Doderer's notion of the *Umweg* ("detour"). The modest and ordinary-extraordinary hero Melzer distinguishes himself by somewhat cumbersome indirectness. After the war Melzer, a lieutenant before and during the First World War, is employed by an office which levies taxes on tobacco products. The time of the action is summer and early autumn of 1925, with frequent excursions into the prewar years, particularly the summer of 1911. Main themes of the novel are the permanence and continuity of human concerns, and on a traditional "heroic" level, the transformation of Melzer into a man who regains what Doderer calls his *Zivilverstand* (civilian mind) and who acts, therefore, in an undogmatic and effective way. The climax of the novel is represented by Melzer's presence at the accident of Mary K., to whom he was once engaged. With assurance and calm he helps to save her from bleeding to death. Kneeling on the street, his hands red with blood, he is suddenly able to act *and* contemplate or remember.

Melzer's slow humanization does not take place by learning the ways of the civilian world; nor is that Doderer's intent. Melzer spends much of his time lying on a bear-rug, making exceedingly strong Turkish coffee, smoking cigarettes and remembering. His memory constantly leaps over the gap caused by the war, and he recalls specific times, dates, encounters, moods, atmospheres, often with little tangible action. One day that stands out with particular clarity, rising involuntarily from the "depth of the years," includes an episode during a bear hunt (Melzer rests on his trophy) which he undertook with a friend, Major Laska, in Bosnia, in the year 1911. Echoing Ruy de Fanez's encounter with the dragon (*Das letzte Abenteuer*) and Count Manuel's mystical experience during the chamois hunt (*Ein Umweg*), Melzer remembers the sights, and particularly the smells, of that day with extraordinary clarity: "So Melzer. . .[was] taking in everything around him with special clarity and sharpness, just as when the picture of a garden comes into a sunny room through freshly cleaned windows" (SHS, 83). *That* he sees is more significant than *what* he sees. Doderer's favorite leitmotif—the window—emphasizes freshly cleaned, unobstructed apperception. During that day Melzer reaches a state of ecstasy.

Doderer refers to a nearly saintly image in describing Melzer's mental condition during the hunt. In his characteristic manner, he takes the world "ecstasy" quite literally as standing outside one's self, being in a trance: "There are states of inner being when we are untied from the pillar of our own self and also rule our body as never before" (SHS, 83). This release from one's own self, with all the tangible details that remind Melzer of this state, remains one of the central "events" in his life. Doderer underscores the fact that Melzer's memory does not focus on memorable events and occupies him *nicht als ein Nennbares* (SHS, 82), like something that cannot (or must not) be named:

. . . but later it trickled forth, innumerable times, in a quiet, hardly recognizable manner; and it gradually spread, deep down there inside of him, and it sent out little streams and flowed together with other images in *ineffable combination.* (SHS, 82, my emphasis)

If anything can be said to contribute to Melzer's final humanization, it is the clear memory of the day of the hunt and its mystical ecstasy, or, as the fine term *Selbstaufgabe* indicates, the readiness and ability to give oneself up and act with increased regard for others. Doderer blends mysticism with Christian concepts of humility and charity, and Melzer has aptly been compared to the fool Parzifal, a model of the Christian drama of quest and salvation.

Melzer, like other positive characters in the novel, distinguishes himself by a high degree of punctiliousness, watchfulness for hollow and overused phrases, and great concern for others. Doderer thereby incorporates the kind of dignity that he considers to be characteristically Austrian—possibly comparable to Spanish bearing—and for which the slightly exaggerated prototype is Councillor Zihal, whose name Doderer transposes into a character trait known as *der höhere Zihalismus austriaco hispanicus* (SHS, 457). Doderer ascribes some eccentric qualities to Melzer and Zihal so that they should not seem pompous, but the significance of the idea of dignity goes to the center of his view that twentieth-century man has lost the authentic dignity that comes naturally from within.

Except at the end, Melzer is also a curiously passive hero. He mainly distinguishes himself, by his ability not to get involved. Nevertheless, Doderer takes great care to relate Melzer's existence to that of almost all other characters in the novel, if not in direct relationships, at least in contiguousness. Melzer is frequently taken along, sometimes quite literally, "for a ride" and deposited next to other characters. His first meeting with Editha Schlinger-Pastré comes about because he happens to meet Rittmeister Eulenfeld, who is showing off his red four-seater automobile. Melzer suddenly finds himself sitting next to a beautiful woman: "He had just been taken along, he was simply put down somewhere and a woman set next to him; and to top it he liked her very much" (SHS, 91). But in spite, or perhaps because, of his passive nature—Melzer serves as a point of intersection for the multitude of characters in the novel.

Together with the *Dingsymbol* of the Strudlhof steps, and the connecting link represented by Melzer, the novel has several other epicenters, among which the action is distributed. The most important are among these: (1) the relationship between Grete Siebenschein and René Stangeler (one of Doderer's alter egos), (2) the group of people meeting in the Villa Stangeler, (3) the group or *troupeau* surrounding Rittmeister Eulenfeld, and (4) the simple people around Zihal.

The lack of linear action and the distribution of the reader's attention to several narrative areas, and the resultant lack of tension in the novel emphasize an important point: *what* happens is not important, but rather *how* it happens; the way toward the goal, rather than the goal itself, is what matters.

In spite of the apparent lack of action and tension, there are occasionally hilarious scenes of intrigue involving Editha Pastré-Schlinger, who, with her German fiancé Wedderkopp, is attempting to smuggle Austrian tobacco products into Germany. The appearance of Editha's identical (except for the scar left by an appendectomy!) twin, the twin's attempts at seducing the reluctant and methodical Melzer, the predictable but delicious possibilities of mistaken identity, and the masterfully baroque language and manner of Eulenfeld all contribute occasionally fast-paced action or heighten the tension of the novel. But the action does not lead anywhere. The affairs of Editha Schlinger-Pastré, the "dilettante in badness" (*Dilettantin in Schlechtigkeiten*), are meaningless. The elaborate machinations and cabals resolve themselves into repentance and harmony, in part because of the gentle and forgiving Melzer, who, in the end, finds out that others have been playing with him, but who rather summarily forgives them all.

Throughout *Die Strudlhofstiege* we follow a multiplicity of contiguous fates, trivial events and encounter crisscrossing social divisions, as well as temporal divisions. Through constant shuttling back and forth in memory from the authorial time (sometime in the 1940s) to the two narrative times (the years 1911 and 1925) Doderer establishes a sense of continuity between the worlds of 1911 and

1925. Although representing an important section of Melzer's life, the war years are deemphasized and the continuity of events and characters, of the unchanging interests of ordinary human beings, is impressed upon the reader. As soon as Melzer is able to enter fully the ordinary world, as soon as he makes a clear commitment to Thea Rokitzer, as soon as he enters Zihal's world, his story is over. Even though the ending may have aspects of an idyll, Doderer seems convinced of the primacy of the ordinary over the extraordinary, as well as of the fact that the quasi-historical aspects of novel writing finds its justification in presenting a social panorama in which individual fates are imbedded. Individual fates thus have greater legitimacy than collective fates.

Nevertheless, the subject of the novel, Melzer's humanization, sometimes seems peripheral. The reason Melzer is not in constant focus is a manifestation of Doderer's belief in defining or revealing character through interaction. Character, so Doderer seems to say, is not merely an accumulation of qualities, rather character is formed and defined within the crisscrossing multiplicity of fates, events, and encounters with other characters. Doderer frequently uses images of weaving to describe the composition of his novels, and we can see in the warp and woof of intersecting lines of fate the theme of *Die Strudlhofstiege*.

In addition to showing character formation through interaction, Doderer uses figures in the novel as foils to each other. Thus Eulenfeld, the veteran Rittmeister, however charming his eccentric language and manners may seem, reveals his essentially evil nature in his interactions. He attempts to manipulate others, to impose himself, to take others along, both literally and figuratively, when he is not paralyzed by drunkenness. Even when they are at leisure Melzer and Eulenfeld reveal their opposing natures. Whereas Eulenfeld loses his capacity to think, Melzer attempts to reach a condition which Doderer refers to as *Denkschlaf* (thinking sleep), semiwaking induced by strong Turkish coffee and tobacco smoked in a chibouk. When he has reached this state, Melzer seems exceptionally aware of specific details of his past. By contrast, Eulenfeld becomes stultified, even "petrified" by alcohol. In contrast to the polished character of Eulenfeld, Melzer's character seems incomplete, but he remains open and accessible. Reinforced by metaphors of openness, the trait of *Zugänglichkeit* is a key ingredient in Doderer's description of positive characters. Being and remaining accessible does not define character, but simply makes character possible.

Doderer's cautious and indirect approach to the theme of character development is skillfully reinforced by the probing and tentative composition of *Die Strudlhofstiege*. He has diffused this theme by embedding character formation in interaction, by carefully calculating the illusion of the absence of linear composition, instead aiming for simultaneity, breadth of action, and a sense of the multiplicity of fates.

In addition to a portrait of a section of Viennese society before and after World War I, Doderer portrayed the always elusive and cometimes mysterious aura of places and persons. The camphor smells of empty rooms in the summer, the green light under the trees surrounding the Strudlhof steps, a vulture circling high in the sky, or the smell of strong coffee and tobacco are a few of the recurring impressions that communicate the texture of physical details. Doderer the novelist and the historian have joined forces.

One aspect of *Die Strudlhofstiege* may seem puzzling: the novel was written during and after Europe's most frightening encounter with totalitarianism. Yet there are almost no references to historical events. Yet the connections between the novel and the times exist. Doderer speaks through René Stangeler, who almost casually refers to the madness of the times (*Wahnsinn der Zeit*). During one of the Turkish coffee inspired conversations between Melzer and Stangeler Doderer reveals through Stangeler what seems to be the deepest intent behind writing *Die Strudlhofstiege*. Viewing war and totalitarianism as a "second reality" Doderer sees his writing as a step in the direction of "first reality" or real being (*wirkliches Sein*, cf. SHS, 686). Doderer has made a statement concerning his time by concentrating on gradual, almost accidental development of character, in implied contrast to character dictated either by clever psychologists or brutal propaganda ministers. He concentrates on a world rich in banal details, endowed with elusive charm and subtle attractions, thereby communicating a sense of real time and place rather than a world designed by aloof and arrogant ideologists. *Die Strudlhofstiege* is an attempt to escape from the horrors of second reality, to search instead for authenticity and individuality of being, the "firm ground of real being" (*der feste Boden des wirklichen Seins*, SHS, 686). The complexity and urgency of this search becomes more intense and direct in *Die Dämonen*.

III Die Dämonen *(The Demons)*

Die Dämonen was published in 1956 on Doderer's sixtieth birthday. This long novel secured Doderer's reputation as one of the major novelists writing in German. It was also his first large work to be translated into English (Alfred A. Knopf, 1961). The reaction from American and English critics was predominantly positive. Frederic Morton, writing in the *New York Times Book Review*, hailed it as a "genuine modern epic,"[6] and, comparing Doderer with Hermann Broch and Robert Musil, he added: "Doderer is less intellectual, more fluid and dramatic than his two predecessors—and more universally valid in his diagnosis of Western culture."[7] Morton praised Doderer's descriptive talents: "Last, but not least among Doderer's troublesome talents, is his eye for social detail. Indefatigable, it moves from the number of pots in a petty-bourgeois kitchen to the moldings in the salon of a count; an eye whose comprehension is exhaustive, exhausting, and continuously significant."[8] Morton referred to the novel as an "Austrian passion play"[9] where good and evil receive their traditional deserts, and he concluded: "Not only the brilliance of his technique, but his moral responsiveness to his material make Doderer the foremost novelist writing in German today. Out of the ambiguous glitter of Vienna between the wars he has drawn the metaphors of his creed. In *The Demons* we have an intricate, passionately conservative, magnificent book."[10]

Orville Prescott, writing in the *New York Times* on September 25, 1961, called *Die Dämonen* "one of the longest and most ambitious European novels of modern times. So complex, so subtle and so intricate in its spiral structure is this enormous work that it defies classification and brief description."[11] In *Newsweek* of October 2, 1961, we read of *Die Dämonen* as a "crowded block-buster"; "[Doderer's] mural is immense—too vast, too considered in detail, too unhurried, perhaps, for American readers."[12] However, George Steiner, in *The Reporter* reacted more critically: "*The Demons* is like one of those vast government buildings erected by the Austro-Hungarian Empire and still in present use; it is monumental, but parts of it seem vacant and have a musty air. . . . Lovers, intellectuals, ex-officers, financiers, scheming widows, bourgeois and workmen drift across Doderer's panorama in bewildering skeins of relation or chance encounter."[13] Steiner considers Doderer's narrator to have a "crotchety, gossipy voice,"[14] calls his social and political references "fantastically parochial," and labels his narrative technique as "fussy and oblique."[15] Steiner closes his remarks with:

"In *The Demons*, Doderer makes of Vienna what perhaps it is: a provincial town with a somewhat pompous and unsavory past. Decked out in lavish design, this dull book leaves one with the image of a whale spouting feebly in the shallows of the brown Danube."[16]

In the *Herald Tribune* of September 24, 1961, Denver Lindley called *Die Dämonen* "a monolithic and carefully wrought work of art. Everything in it has been thought out, planned, arranged. Even the reader has not been forgotten: the vast array of characters is introduced, reintroduced, labelled and commented upon until they become more easily recognizable than one's neighbors."[17]

Writing in *Books Abroad*, Ivar Ivask sees *Die Dämonen* as the completion of a trilogy which had begun with *Zihal*, and was continued with *Die Strudlhofstiege*. As such, he argues it is one of *the* literary events in German letters for the following reasons:

(1) Doderer's is the most successful synthesis so far of the idealism of the German *Bildungsroman* with the realism of the European social novel; (2) He has proved the continued vitality of the classical novel of psychological realism simply by integrating into it various modern techniques; (3) He confronts the present realistically instead of writing a historical, surrealist, or mythological parable of escape, and he accomplishes this not by resorting to the drab *Zeitroman*, but rather by aiming at poetical transformations of his age into sharp, memorable images and psychologically believable characters; (4) Since he is one of the truly convincing realists in the German novel, he may enter Vienna on the map of the European novel as the only other German city there besides Lübeck; (5) He is one of the few genuine humorists among German novelists; (6) Doderer's may well be the most penetrating of women characters in the German novel (although it has been an Austrian *forte* for some time); and (7) Last but not least, on account of his extremely rich vocabulary and ability to render shades of individual speech.[18]

Obviously the reactions of critics and commentators abound and vary. Most recent Doderer criticism (Hans Joachim Schröder, Trommler, Reininger) tends to be somewhat skeptical of Doderer's "passion-play," recognizing that the struggle between light and dark, good and evil, reality and nonreality, needs perhaps somewhat more cautious treatment than we find in *Die Dämonen*.

Die Dämonen is one of the most kaleidoscopic novels written in German. Like *Die Strulhofstiege*, it has various epic-centers, all contiguous to the main theme: the decline of a society, ending in the "Cannae of Austrian freedom" (ThD, 1311), juxtaposed with the positive development of individual fates, such as that of Leonhard

Kakabsa. The characters may contribute collectively to society's decline, or they may stand by passively; they may simply be caught up in their daily existence or they may undergo significant development. But from the beginning ("Overture") it is clear that the time span chosen by Doderer is fraught with historical significance. The demonic terror is symbolized by the burning of the Palace of Justice by an angry mob, in Vienna, on July 15, 1927, and foreshadows subsequent and much more terrible events. Doderer takes the reader to the years 1925 - 27 as a prelude to events to come.

Die Dämonen is not a historical novel in the sense that it narrates with the benefit of hindsight but, through the use of fictitious chronicles and chroniclers, it portrays the past as if it were present time. Nevertheless, the reader remains vaguely aware of the authorial time plane of the 1950s.

One of the most complex and important aspects of *Die Dämonen* is its structure. Dietrich Weber, in his monograph on Doderer, has succeeded in elucidating the significance of the interplay of structure and meaning. In part, the various time levels constitute different narrative modes. The time of narration furthest removed from the actual events falls into the year 1955. This temporal distance helps the narrator to the past with all its implications. Another time plane is constituted by the chronicles of Geyrenhoff, written down shortly after the main events, and stretching from 1926 to shortly after the burning of the Palace of Justice. The third time plane is established through the numerous sections or chapters that tell of events in the present time when the narrating chronicler (Doderer in the guise of Geyrenhoff) or the narrator (Doderer) disappears behind omniscient narration.

Although there is only one narrating *I*, the novel is an "edited" composite of descriptions or contributions from several figures within the novel. The narrative *I* is almost always that of Geyrenhoff, but, as mentioned before, an omniscient author watches over Geyrenhoff, taking him to task when he becomes too involved in the action and loses the detachment which is thought necessary for a chronicler.[19]

The tension between chronicle and novel, or between objective, detached description and novelistic penetration of events and characters, is not only a structural problem of *Die Dämonen* but also one of its many themes: How can the real world best be portrayed? The initial *desideratum*, at least during the first phase of Doderer's work on the novel's first part in the 1930s, was that of the objective witness, the calm and reasonable teller of events, Councillor

Geyrenhoff, who, perched high above Vienna in a painter's studio, has retired into a comfortable leisurely bachelor's existence. Portraying the activities of a group of friends and acquaintances, he also solicits and receives from his friends reports which he edits and integrates into his chronicle, thus adding insights and viewpoints to which he would otherwise not be privy.

Geyrenhoff, a kind, and concerned man, rather than a man of action, seems to be the ideal spectator. Nevertheless, however little action there is in the novel, Geyrenhoff finds himself drawn into events. He falls in love with the beautiful and rich widow Friederike Ruthmayr and also becomes involved in the one thread of action that runs through the entire novel, the clarification of Quapp's fate, especially the embezzlement of her paternal inheritance by Levielle. Quapp, whose given name is Charlotte, is the half-sister of Kajetan von Schlaggenberg, one of Geyrenhoff's closest friends and collaborators, a novelist and former journalist and one of several alter egoes for Heimito von Doderer. Through the intervention of Geyrenhoff, and with the help of the old soldier Alois Gach, the embezzlement schemes of Levielle are thwarted, and Quapp inherits her father's money. Her story, like so many others, ends in a married idyll.

Although Doderer's handling of Geyrenhoff has also been criticized, it seems nonetheless to increase the richness and fascination of the novel. There is little controversy, however, among critics on the inclusiveness and broad sweep of the novel's manifold actions. However bewildering the various actions may seem, Doderer does relate them in a most painstaking, although not immediately evident, manner to the historical background. In the "Overture," written from the fictional viewpoint of 1955, he stresses the horror of the unfolding historical events:

Terrible things took place in my native land and in this, my native city, at a time long after the grave and lighthearted stories I wish to relate here had come to an end. And one thing that lay curled and amorphous and germinal within the events that I must recount emerged, dripping blood, took on a name, became visible to the eye which had been almost blinded by the vortex of events, shot forth, and was, even in its beginnings, recognizable—gruesomely inconspicuous and yet distinctly recognizable for what it was. (ThD, 17)

In this passage we see clearly Doderer's intention to write a novel with historical dimensions, to portray the demonic "thing" carefully and in detail. It follows also that the stories had to be "grave *and* lighthearted" (*ernst und heiter*). Even the most murderous villainy has a human dimension, and while the reader may not exactly admire the physical agility of a burglar in *Die Dämonen* about to murder someone, one of the prostitutes who is watching this burglar climb along fragile ledges to his victim, gawks in utter fascination. We may certainly pass judgment, but Doderer does not provide us with facile guidelines for such judgments.

Doderer's approach to historical events is signalled by an image that he cites three times in the "Overture": life is compared to a woven texture, and, in order to portray life or a section of history, one may grasp a single thread at any random point and manage to reach and affect the entire texture. Doderer places emphasis not only on the interpretation of events at a given time and place, but also on the novelist's freedom to begin his portrayal anywhere. However random the beginning may seem, it must sooner or later lead to the other events. If historical reality does not make connections evident, the mind of the remembering author must relate all events, however distant they may seem from one another. Eventually—and this requires some patience on the part of the reader—we will perceive the entire historical texture.

It is in this specific sense that the first chapter (after the "Overture") is entitled *Draussen am Rande*, which would be best translated as "At the Periphery," rather than "On the Outskirts of the City," as in the existing translation. By beginning his narrative at the periphery of the city and thus of the main events, Doderer stresses the equivalence of all characters and events. Thus the opening scene, with Dr. Dwight Williams, famous lepidopterist from Buffalo, N.Y., who is sitting on a little island in a stream in the Vienna Woods with beautiful Emma Drobil, is peripheral in terms of geography, as well as in those of the plot.

Nevertheless, although Williams and Drobil remain at the periphery, multiple connections to more central characters do exist. While staying in London, Williams has lived in the house of Madame Libesny, who in turn knew Mary K., and even had a portrait of the latter hanging in her room. By introducing Mary K., Doderer establishes a connection with *Die Strudlhofstiege*, where she was one of the central figures. For Williams, anticipation of the meeting with Mary K. becomes quite important. It is also another instance (comparable to the one in *Ein Mord den jeder begeht*) where a picture is surrounded by an irresistible aura, to which a male character is mysteriously attracted.

Even further connections are established in the first few pages.

The maid of Madame Libesny happens to be the sister of one of the major figures in the novel, Leonhard Kakabsa. London is also the place where Camy von Schlaggenberg flees from her unhappy marriage with Kajetan. The multiple connections emerge gradually but clearly, and we are immediately introduced to some of the major locales and characters.

The opening of this otherwise thoroughly urban novel in the Vienna Woods has yet another function. It gives Doderer the opportunity to broaden the novel's perspective to the East. In his characteristic attempt to find parallels between landscape and mind he sees Vienna as open to the influences of both East and West, similar to the world(s) of Thomas Mann's *The Magic Mountain*. The very topography of the landscape symbolizes this openness. In the Vienna Woods one senses and sees the nearness of the plateaus that continue into Hungary and from there to the steppes of Asia. In a sense, the edge of the Vienna Woods is seen as the interface between the ordered and rational, West, and the expansive, continuous, emotional East: ". . .[The Vienna Woods] are a farewell to the pleasant, cozy western individuality and smaller land-masses; in a way they are a farewell to the compactness of Greece, standing as they do close by the portals to the East, to immoderate expanses" (ThD, 29). Doderer's fascination with the East, which he shares with a number of German writers, among them Rilke and Werfel, is based on the belief in spirituality, brotherhood, emotion and irrationality, holiness and salvation as characteristics of the East. Later on, Doderer freed himself from overly mythicizing the East, in part because of his increasingly critical views concerning the Russian revolution and subsequent political events in Russia (cf. *Tangenten*).

The first chapter of *Die Dämonen* also includes a brief description of Mary K.'s *aristeia*, her brave struggle to learn to walk with one artificial leg. By using the Homeric term referring to the great struggles portrayed in the *Iliad*, Doderer lifts Mary K. to the stature of a heroic figure. The secret of her heroism lies in her ability to accept *what is*, rather than to moan about how such a horrid accident was possible. Through her acceptance of reality she obtains strength to overcome her handicap. Her pride and her beauty as a woman are thus immeasurably enhanced.

After almost parenthetically sketching the connections of Mary K. with Grete Siebenschein, the fiancée of René von Stangeler, Doderer returns to Williams and Drobil, exploring the outskirts and suburbs of Vienna and slowly introducing the reader—literally coming from the outside—to the city of Vienna.

After beginning on the periphery, the narrative "I" of Geyrenhoff resumes the narration and begins to tell of the coincidental move of a group of friends to a particularly beautiful district in Vienna. Döbling. *Die Unsrigen* "our crowd" develops around Geyrenhoff and Quapp. The number of characters portrayed is gradually increased and the texture of the novel is broadened. We become familiar with the details of Schaggenberg's disastrous marriage and follow one of Rittmeister Eulenfeld's spontaneous and far-flung drinking tours. During these tours, which (the German) Eulenfeld leads with his red sports car, friends and acquaintances are "kidnapped" from their homes, from the street, or from cafés. One of the first of these outings touches the stately mansion of Friederike Ruthmayr, who happens to stand near a balcony while some prankish members of the tour climb up and hand her a cognac bottle from which "it is said" she actually drank. This, like so many episodes, not only serves to bring "our crowd" closer together, but—feigning reportorial uncertainty—reinforces the tentativeness of the point of view of the narration.

From chapter to chapter, Doderer broadens the scope of his narrative. With never diminishing attention to detail and unprejudiced compassion and understanding, the narrator takes us from the daytime meetings of a group of wealthy and mostly corpulent ladies in a fashionable café to the opera box of Friederike Ruthmayr, and finally to the nocturnal raucous activities in a dive called Café Kaunitz. We are also introduced to Leonhard Kakabsa and witness his encounters with himself in a characteristically indirect way: Lying on his leather couch, Kakabsa smells the various odors wafting into his room, in part from barges that move along the Danube, and he suddenly realizes his own sensitivity to the associative of smells. Just as Doderer was fascinated by smells and the sense of smell as a direct, if primitive, way of perceiving the environment, so Kakabsa suddenly asks himself: "What the devil was I born for—to smell things?" (ThD, 121); and he soon answers himself with an unequivocal "Yes." Smelling has a "veracity. . .beyond question" (ThD, 122), and it stands for a direct, truthful, and unalterable way of perceiving reality.

Giving a simple positive answer to this apparently outlandish question is only the beginning of Kakabsa's development. A significant impulse comes from a chance encounter with the daughter of a bookseller, and the seemingly random purchase of a Latin grammar. Doderer criticism often treats the story of the factory worker Kakabsa, who learns Latin, eventually becomes the private librarian of a rich Count, and wins the heart and hand of beautiful Mary K. as a slightly embarrassing case of success or self-improvement, a kind of bootstrap program à la Doderer. But, as Wendelin Schmidt-Dengler and others have shown, Doderer attempts inconspicuously to portray the growth of Kakabsa's awareness of the importance of language not *qua* language, but as a way of establishing contact with reality.[20] Only adequately supple and thorough knowledge and use of language can enable us to perceive, let alone portray, reality in all its elusiveness. Kakabsa's particular and indirect approach via Latin underlines Doderer's conviction that language is important as part of a historical and changing continuum. Language is in part a theme of the story of Kakabsa. By emancipating himself from the metalanguage of his local dialect, he emancipates himself as a person. In addition, the accidental nature of the turning points (smells and Latin) in Kakabsa's life reminds us of mystical moments in the lives of characters in other Doderer narratives.

If Kakabsa's story is one of success, it is not only because he learns to read Pico dela Mirandola in Latin, and because he rises from the world of the proletariat, but also because he lifts himself from the anonymous mass and becomes a "free" individual. He recapitulates the process of humanization (*Menschwerdung*), which is central to Doderer's thinking. Humanization implies self-sufficiency, autonomy of judgment, uncluttered perception of people and events, and always a degree of loneliness. In *Die Dämonen*, Kakabsa can be contrasted with most other characters, who fail in a more or less dramatic way. Their failure is constituted by a tendency to fall prey to anonymous mass desires, mass movements, or ideologies; by a tendency toward laziness, an obsession with whims, and finally, deficient individuation. These characters and tendencies constitute the demonic aspect that Doderer alludes to in the "Overture." The story of the Gadarene swine, which Dostoyevsky used as a motto to *The Possessed* (translated into German as *Die Dämonen*), is only faintly recognizable in the obsessions of various characters. To be sure, in spite of their occasional brilliance, their flashes of wit and insight, most of the characters, from whores and handimen to the members of high nobility and high finance, are blind to the senseless and murderous political moods that culminate in the burning of the Palace of Justice described in the magnificent chapter "The Fire."

The theme of the novel eludes the reader because *Die Dämonen* is not the story of any one character. Doderer's attempt to write a "total novel" implies the lack of a simple, monographic theme. As Dietrich Weber succinctly puts it: "The total novel is—strictly speaking—a novel without a theme" (DW, 181). However, just as totality and artistic limitations are paradoxes that cannot be resolved, so themes manage to emerge from *Die Dämonen*. Weber summarizes the development of the novel by viewing Doderer's initial main theme as that of "second reality," first and most simply exemplified by Schlaggenberg's antiideology of the "Fat Females." Schlaggenberg is angry at the popular preference for a skin-and-bones ideal of feminine beauty and reacts with adulation of a somewhat lopsided opposite. As the ideological architect constructs an ideal political state, so Schlaggenberg creates an ideal (fat) woman.

Another variation of the theme of second reality is the anti-Semitism of Viennese society. The creation of racial stereotypes is, in Doderer's terms, a tendency to accept a false, second reality, and remain blind to the true, first reality. An interesting twist given by Doderer to the genesis of totalitarian ideologies lies in his theory that totalitarian, as well as revolutionary, ideology springs from basic mistakes in, or failures of, perception. Through laziness, stupidity, irony, through *Apperzeptions-Verweigerung* (refusal to perceive openly), totalitarianism is given the opportunity to establish itself. Constructs of thought, rather than from apperception, are mistaken for truth and, in Doderer's terms, "second reality" obscures "first reality." The Nazi regime and the Second World War became for Doderer excursions into a collective, totalitarian "second" reality, against which the individual was helpless, and which had to be suffered until its inevitable demise. The collapse of Nazism signaled the return to "first reality," and Doderer adjusted to it with speed, spontaneity, and relief.

Doderer however, does not absolve the individual from responsibility. The demons alluded to in the title are the forces of collectivism, totalitarianism, anti-Semitism, antihumanism, and, in general, of blindness (again, *Apperceptions-Verweigerung*), yet each is modeled on individual concrete examples, most of which are neither obvious nor pernicious.

One of the most conspicuous representatives of people falling prey to primitive urges is Jan Herzka (familiar from *Die Bresche*), with his sexual aberrations and phantasies. Herzka has inherited an old castle, and in the manuscript collection of the castle's library Stangeler, the young historian, finds a codex containing precisely what Herzka had wished for: a description of the capture of two women by the lord of the castle (Herzka's ancestor) and their spurious trial as witches. Fascinated with watching women in the pose of naked martyrs, the historical lord of the castle sees to it that no harm is done to the women. However, he encourages two of his servants who are charged with administering the punishment and with watching the women, to seduce (or be seduced by) the women. He succeeds on all counts, and in the end the women are released "unharmed." The author of the manuscript is, in the end, relieved and realizes that he has lived through a phantasmagoria, a kind of second reality. Afterwards he notes: "And me seemeth I have ben made ayen whole oute of two halfe men, and the one half was of wode" (ThD, 816). As the young author becomes "whole" again, so Jan Herzka adjusts his phantasies to his bourgeois existence. Nevertheless, private ideologies and superimposition of preconceived types serve as miniature replicas of historically significant movements. But Herzka remains blind to the end. This blindness, multiplied a thousand-fold, makes possible the "terrible events" Doderer describes in the "Overture."

The political events described in the novel are consistently understated and can easily be overlooked. There are, however, the Hungarian nationalists meeting in a hut near the Austro-Hungarian border, singing their haunting songs, telling tales of adventure, and lightly touching on the trustworthiness of this or that character in the pursuit of the Cause. There is the senseless killing of an invalid and his ten-year-old nephew in the cross-fire between socialist and fascist factions; and the subsequent trial and verdict of the *Volksgericht* (People's Court) freeing the murderers is reached on July 14, 1927, one day before the burning of the Palace of Justice. These events are not coincidental, but Doderer treats them with a lightness that avoids either reportage or ideology-laden journalism. His treatment suffices, however, to reinforce the irony of a rebellion of the people against a verdict of the court of the people.

Events, such as the killing of the invalid Mathias Csmarits and his nephew Pepi Grössing, contain historical, personal, and demonic aspects. Csmarits happens to be the brother of one of the most remarkable figures in the novel, Frau Anna Kapsreiter, known as Kaps; and the little boy who is killed is her nephew, whom she has loved with uncritical abandon. Kaps is remarkable because of her fears and dreams, recorded in "Kaps's Night Book," which constitutes two brief but powerful chapters in the novel. Not only does Kaps discourse on her fears for the life of her nephew, who has to accompany his father wherever he goes in a strife-torn country, but her diary also records her dreams, which reflect much more pervasive anxieties. She writes down phantasies stimulated by bits and pieces she has heard or seen in cheap little magazines. Her nightmares constitute the unscientific parallel to the cogitations of Dwight Williams concerning the possible or reported existence of giant squid. In the end, the escapade of Meisgeier and Didi, the murderer and the whore, into the sewers of Vienna, together with Kaps's nightmares and Williams's speculations, form a texture of horror which exists in a literal and metaphorical subterranean realm. In Kaps's "Night Books," the evil force is referred to as a *Kastl-Kubi*, an ingenuous term for a threatening imaginary creature who combines aspects of Kaps's brother (whom she blames for the death of her nephew) and—due to the allusion to *Kubus*, or better *Incubus*—the essence of the demonic. Even the fire of the burning Palace of Justice is anticipated in Kaps's dreams. Doderer makes quite clear the connection between her dream and the actual fire by choosing the same word *ein rotes Wimmerl* for Kaps's "Night Book" and for Geza von Orkay's description of the actual fire as seen from the safe distance of the Cobenzl (cf. DD 1205, 1292).

The culmination of the novel in the chapter "The Fire" is directly preceded by one of Kaps's haunting nightmares. In "The Fire," Doderer places great emphasis on achieving a high degree of simultaneity and—if only by implication—of equivalence. The activities of all the main characters of the novel are reported in rapidly shifting scenes or episodes, one following the other without transition. On this fateful day, the whereabouts of counts, scholars, workers, pimps, and whores is surveyed. The uproar, the rioting, the fire, and the mass hysteria force themselves upon everyone's attention. And it is the reaction of the various figures that typifies and marks them as either "free" individuals or "unfree" hangers-on. It might be Doderer's paradigmatic assertion that freedom consists of the choice between joining the mob (the *Ruass*) which riots senselessly or staying away. In this particular situation, there is really no other choice. The nonrational demonic forces of the rabble can hardly be opposed, except by an organized and equally terrifying force. The free individual seems to have only the choice of nonparticipation. As mentioned earlier, it is part of Doderer's philosophy that one cannot counter a phenomenon on its own level. Thus, ideology, having become frenetic and mindless, cannot effectively be countered by an opposing ideology. In this particular instance, withdrawal remains the only feasible response.

The chapter "The Fire" opens with an intense evocation of an aura of darkness, silence, and anticipation. Again, as in the beginning of the novel, Doderer approaches his subject from the periphery, through the description of mountains and woods outside the city. The noise made by a little lizard hiding under dry leaves emphasizes the silence, and a whistle from the depth of the dark woods takes on a haunting quality. With the intrusion of the early morning sun into the small alleys of the city, Doderer gradually approaches the scenes of the day's important events. The rising sun and the slowly increasing intensity of the songs of birds, even the awakening of some ducks, is described with Homeric leisureliness and specificity.

In about thirty-seven short episodes Doderer touches upon the activities of the major characters in what seems to be a minute-by-minute account. After the atmospheric beginning, Quapp (Charlotte von Schlaggenberg) is described as waking up, thinking of her new lover and future husband, and reviewing her newly acquired fortune. From her the focus switches to Anny Gräven, a prostitute, waking up with a sense of relief that she has been spared a hangover from the previous night's drinking. Soon her corpulent friend Anita stops by to invite her to go to town, where unusual things seem to be happening. Next we see Leonhard Kakabsa rising in the Palais Croix, where he now works as a librarian. The subsequent episode describes a group of young people (*Kajetans Bande*) who have been prompted to break in at Levielle's to retrieve some important documents to help reveal certain embezzlement schemes. Then Doderer switches back to Leonhard, who is now entering the university library, and, in contrast, comes across a treatise on human dignity at about the same time when the beginning riots come close to the university. Then the scene shifts to Geyrenhoff, who rises and proceeds to breakfast with his old colleague Gürtzner-Gontard. Subsequently, René von Stangeler goes to meet a professor from Harvard who shares his interest in medieval historiography. And in the tenth episode, Generaldirektor Küffer picks up a group of youngsters for a swimming party at his house in the suburbs later during the day.

The eleventh episode brings us to a high point in the chapter. Geyrenhoff is observing some of the rioting through a pair of binoculars from Gürtzner-Gontard's room. He watches the killing of an old woman who had been carrying milk bottles in a shopping net. As she lies there, a random victim of the riots—it is unclear whether the bullets of the rioters or of the police have killed her—milk and blood, red and white, Austria's national colors, and metaphors for youth in many a fairy tale, run together in the street. Geyrenhoff notes the fateful symbolism: "Call it splitting hairs if you like. . . .for me that fall of the colors, inextricably linked with the old woman who lay face down, shot to death—that was what brought home to me the gravity and irrevocability of what was happening on July 15, 1927" (ThD, 1230).

From their window, Gürtzner-Gontard and Geyrenhoff can observe a section of the mob surrounding the Palace of Justice. Among those addressing the crown is Imre von Gyurkicz, cartoonist and painter, and former lover of Quapp. Gyurkicz is also associated with Hungarian Nationalism and is Geyrenhoff's friend. As he is urging the crowd to riot, the police apparently are advancing, and shots ring out. Everyone vanishes from Geyrenhoff's view except Imre, who lies there dead. Geyrenhoff considers Imre's death "the restoration of his honor, the healing of his deepest injury, the elimination of his most secret shame" (ThD, 1234). Perhaps that shame is grounded in Imre's non-committed and toying response to problems of politics and to the needs of Charlotte von Schlaggenberg. Nevertheless, his death is no apotheosis, but rather a "miserable death," leaving Geyrenhoff to muse about the "celerity" with which "the mechanism of life can conclude any biography" (ThD, 1234).

After this scene of public and political events, Doderer switches—without any decrease in emphasis or interest—to the private world, in this instance the apartment of Mary K., who is expecting a visit from Leonhard Kakabsa later that day, and whose upstairs neighbor, Grete Siebenschein, has come to help her cook. The focus shifts back to the hotel where René von Stangeler and the Harvard professor are perusing an old manuscript on medieval witch hunts, both scholars being hardly aware that something significant (electricity failing and phones out of order) is going on outside. From there we are suddenly transported into a changing booth at poolside where corpulent Frau Frauenholzer is squeezing herself into a bathing suit. Next comes a short sketch of adolescent sexual games and the aberrations of Mary K.'s daughter Trix, and then, almost exactly at noon, Doderer switches back to the riots. Significantly, in episode sixteen the "insignificant" prostitute Anny Gräven becomes fed up with the destructive and senseless activities and regains her personal freedom and dignity simply by walking away and returning to her apartment. Her response is a model of normalcy and sanity.

The next two scenes again involve Quapp, who reads and thinks of her new life with new wealth and a husband. Later she walks aimlessly, around the city, only to be plucked out of the chaos and danger by her future husband Geza von Orkay in his diplomatic staff car, and whisked to the outskirts of the city through the sounds of streetfighting. From the safe distance of the Café Cobenzl, Geza and Quapp can observe the fire in the city.

Episode nineteen tells of the grotesque and macabre subterranean journey of the murderer Meisgeier, who with the barmaid Anna Diwald (Didi), sets out to trip policemen from underneath the grate of a sewer. Moving along the sewers of Vienna, in part by boat, they find their way to a busy street. But after a few policemen stumble and fall, one police lieutenant fires his pistol into the sewer, killing both Meisgeier and Didi. Not only is the description of the demonic fascination Meisgeier holds for Didi paradigmatic for the unfreedom of all who go along and for all who do not exercise their free will and individual judgment, but it also demonstrates the logical conclusion that Didi's fascination with evil, which she does not clearly recognize as such, brings about her death. It does occur to her during the walk through the sewers that she could have chosen not to go along, but she lacks the will—rather than the opportunity—to do so.

In the next, the twentieth, episode, Doderer returns to the perspective of Geyrenhoff and to the sage Councillor Gürtzner-Gontard and describes a scene that becomes symbolic for the *non-sense* of the riots. Young men uproot a huge lamp post, and Geyrenhoff fails for a while to see the practical reason for this action: the post is the foundation of a strong barricade. He interprets the episode as a symbolic event representative of a break in the continuity of daily existence, whereas the destruction of the street lighting stands for the darkening of the minds of the masses. Such thoughtless action furnishes yet another example of *Apperzeptions-Verweigerung*. Something irrational and evil drives people to the point where they simply do not want to see. Geyrenhoff even thinks that the rabble might just as well have destroyed the church steeples from which the bells mark the divisions of time.

Doderer underscores the quality of not wanting to see by describing the human embryo covering its eyes with its hands: "the embryo that refused to see the light, that did not want to see life and the continuity of everyday" (*den hingestreckten Alltag*) (ThD, 1259).

Lest it be thought that Doderer is unequivocally on the side of the conservative forces, it must be mentioned that he makes a clear distinction between the *Ruass* (lit., "the soot") and its criminal behavior, and the decent socialists. As Councillor Gontard observes, "That sort of thing has nothing in common with socialism" (ThD, 1261).

During mid-afternoon of the fifteenth of July, the shooting in the streets reaches its peak. From the apartment of Gontard, Geyrenhoff can see only groups of running people against a background of incessant shooting. During a lull in the fighting, Geyrenhoff suddenly remembers his own emotional ties to Friederike Ruthmayr and ceases to be a detached observer and reporter. The world of politics and his personal realm are briefly concentrated in a juxtaposition of smells: "Into my nostrils, filled with the feeble but raw and menacing smell of burning, entered the delicate scent of camphor. And it was the stronger power. . . . I wanted to reach Friederike" (ThD, 1263). As Geyrenhoff leaves the shelter of Gontard's house, the door is locked behind him with two audible turns of the key.

In his attempt to remain faithful to the complexity of events, Doderer interjects an apparently unrelated episode: Frau Mayrinker, occupant of the apartment of the late Frau Kapsreiter, cooking fruit to make preserves, and in the course of her work successfully battles a fire in her kitchen.

Dietrich Weber devotes an entire chapter to this banal scene and concludes that it furnishes an example of Doderer's technique for achieving simultaneity, and for emphasizing the depth and complexity of the world portrayed in his novel. Disparate elements appear next to each other, and since there is no simple theme, formula, or idea under which every episode of the novel can be subsumed, the Frau Mayrinker episode may be seen as an example of Doderer's acceptance of *what is:* During a day that may be the "Cannae of Austrian freedom" a woman puts up preserves. And Doderer does not seem to judge one event to be intrinsically more interesting than another.

To be sure, the Frau Mayrinker episode is analogous to the chapter "The Fire," within which it takes place. The contrast between the conflagration in the city and the fire in Frau Mayrinker's kitchen yields examples for events of greater or lesser complexity. Nevertheless, the historical event and the simple or banal one occur simultaneously. Doderer draws attention to the connection between the personal and the historical spheres when he describes Frau Mayrinker's walk through a part of the city. On the way to a restaurant, feeling exhausted and hungry, she is startled: "The sky was aglare with flames, She started with terrible fright; for a moment, in her weakness and exhaustion, all her happiness collapsed. . . . She could not for some time separate that fire over there from the little fire in her kitchen which had long since been extinguished" (ThD, 1271).

As Weber points out, the Frau Mayrinker episode "is and remains a real scene; on the whole it is neither a model nor a symbol, neither parable nor analog or an abbreviated picture of the whole; it may briefly take on these functions, it does contain them, but it does not exhaust itself in them" (DW, 256). In the final analysis, Doderer uses the episode to assert the primacy of the real over the symbolic. This humorous, banal, and yet serious scene constitutes an illustration of Doderer's goal as a novelist: Since the 1920s he had speculated and theorized about his particular penchant for realistic portrayal. In seeing reality first and foremost as tangible, hard, irreducible stuff for his writing, he departs from what he mockingly calls the German tradition of the "trans-real" novel. For Doderer the everyday, banal world is not merely a cipher, a symbol, or something that must be transcended, but rather *the* authentic reality. Doderer thus establishes himself as one of the few genuine realists in German literature.

The Frau Mayrinker episodes constitute the culmination of "The Fire." The remainder of the chapter concentrates on bringing together four couples: Leonhard Kakabsa and Mary K., Geza von Orkay and Quapp, Geyrenhoff and Friederike Ruthmayr, René Stangeler and Grete Siebenschein. Two brief scenes deal with Stangeler's friend Neuberg, who finally overcomes the trauma of the break-up of his engagement, and, after moving into a new apartment, begins concentrating with gusto and determination on his work as a historian. Even the activities of the more peripheral characters are briefly touched upon. Rittmeister Eulenfeld wanders toward Grinzing with his friend Dr. Körger. Eulenfeld steps into a café and gets stone drunk. Doderer's portrayal of the tolerant atmosphere of a Viennese café is illustrated by the reaction of the waiter. Eulenfeld falls asleep, sitting upright, quiet and well-behaved (*magister equitum petrificatus*). When his friend leaves him and asks the waiter to look after Eulenfeld, the solicitous man comments: "No need to be concerned, Herr Doktor. . . . The Herr Baron frequently has himself a little nap here. We take the liberty of waking him when it's nearly closing time. Usually the Herr Baron likes to have a couple of sausages at that hour" (ThD, 1326). Unfortunately, the translation cannot do justice to the suppleness of *ein kleines Schlaferl,* or the gentility of *in geziemender Façon zu wecken.*

The description of the day of rioting ends with an idyllic scene at the Palais Ruthmayr, where Geyrenhoff, Friederike, Geza, and Quapp meet. Through the revelation of Quapp's background—she is the illegitimate daughter of Friederike's late husband—she is brought even closer to Geyrenhoff and Friederike. But in spite of the personal idylls, the background of the fire remains visible. After a brief rain, the burning Palace of Justice illuminates the thunderclouds, and again Doderer stresses the conflicting smells, which juxtapose two important principles: civilization and demonic destructiveness. "I took a deep breath of the damp air, perfumed by luxuriant plant growth—still with a lingering consciousness of the cool camphor fragrance of the lower part of the salon, through which we had just passed. But the smell that followed immediately afterwards, borne on a barely palpable breeze, came from the towering red flames: the implacable smell of fire" (ThD, 1311). Doderer does not leave the reader with the impression of the idyll, of the detached patricians watching slightly unsavory history from the safety of their palais. The two final episodes in the chapter deal with the fate of Anny Gräven, the kind prostitute, once a friend of Leonhard Kakabsa. After the bodies of Meisgeier and Anna Diwald are pulled out of the sewer shaft, the complicity of Anny Gräven in a murder committed by Meisgeier becomes clear, and she is jailed for six months. But even her story ends on a positive, albeit melancholy note. After she has served her time, she finds that her apartment has been kept for her and the rent paid by some of her friends and clients. The words of the concièrge belie Doderer's hatred for this "species." Herr Ladstätter welcomes her back from jail, asks no questions, reassures her that all is well, orders her apartment warmed up. Anny finds her apartment well stocked with wine, cognac, cigarettes, candy, and cosmetics. After some rest she is back at the side of a client riding to a restaurant for dinner. In this way, Doderer stresses the continuum of normalcy, of even slightly sleazy human affairs.

The last chapter of *Die Dämonen* is devoted to three events: Leonhard Kakabsa's early-morning departure to visit Mary K., Schlaggenberg's return to Vienna from a visit to London, where he has briefly attempted a reconciliation with his wife, Camy, and, finally, the last meeting of "our crowd" at the railroad station, where some of the main characters meet to bid farewell to Quapp and her husband, who are leaving for Switzerland.

The final episode is replete with melcancholy. Geyrenhoff anticipates that he will not see any of his old friends again, "never again in this life" (ThD, 1329). This closing touch of sadness is made even more poignant by a brief paragraph, ostensibly written twenty-eight years later, in 1955, which tells of the death of Friederike

Apogee

Ruthmayr, and of the destruction of her palais during the war. In this manner, the narrator Geyrenhoff once more underscores his temporal distance from the main events which he has just chronicled.

Leonhard Kakabsa's departure to visit Mary K. stresses the mood of beginning, of newness, and of freshness. The imagery surrounding Kakabsa suggests a hero's journey. Thus, while the song of the birds ceases at the moment of the sunrise, Doderer writes: "During that general pause the sky broke open like the husk of a fruit, giving birth to the glowing god. And already he was there above the dark ridges of the mountains, his strength concentrated as it never is in the later hours of the day, which he illuminates in a more disperse fashion" (ThD, 1319).

But the most significant portion of the last chapter tells of the destruction of the "second reality" which has surrounded Kajetan von Schlaggenberg, and thus of his potential for humanization. After the encounter with his estranged wife, Camy, in London, Schlaggenberg strolls along Cheyne Walk and suddenly realizes that his perception of events and people has been clouded: "I instantly recognized the condition in which I'd lived for so long. That condition now dropped away from me. Camy had amputated it for me. It was a condition in which even facts ceased to convince. Because they were not even perceived. That was how I had been living" (ThD, 1326 - 27).

The change in Schlaggenberg's perceptions may strike us as contrived. Nevertheless it falls into the category of sudden unmotivated insights which occur to many of Doderer's heroes. Schlaggenberg's memory focuses suddenly on a little girl he had seen during a ski outing with "our crowd." Now, years later, he suddenly recognizes the identity of the little girl, who is the daughter of Councillor Gürtzner-Gontard. No special significance is attached to her identity. Doderer uses rather the failure in perception, and the sudden recognition from a retrospect of many years, as a metaphor for development and sudden change, for the inexplicable timing of a significant insight, and for the importance of memory for such a change. Schlaggenberg observes: "Getting back on [*das Einrasten*, lit., "clicking in"] took the form of an observation which I made in retrospect. —I hadn't made it at the proper time" (ThD, 1326).

One of the observations we may make concerning the metamorphosis of Schlaggenberg (and other Doderer heroes) is that they are usually prepared for their decisive moment by blindness, or suffering, and that the absence of exhaustive motivation for such a change implies that salvation seems to be an aspect of inevitable fate.

Translating his newly found perceptiveness into tangible action, Schlaggenberg leaves London for Stuttgart to a sign a contract with his publisher. Doderer clearly means to say that Schlaggenberg is cured of his obsessive thinking, of his pseudo-ideology of the "fat females," and that he will be able to resume his writing. Thus obsessive thought (ideology) cedes to unobstructed apperception. Schlaggenberg's particular demons (imposition of thought on life) are exorcised by the acceptance of the vitality and recalcitrance of the world as it is.

The content or meaning of this rich, multifaceted, and even mysterious novel, cannot be summarized, but a passage from Doderer's "Nachtbuch" may be appropriate in conclusion:

. . .I lie as if buried and I am everywhere like earth under the teeming mass of the city, which I have drawn over me like a blanket: this is the genesis and the function of *Die Dämonen*.[21]

CHAPTER 5

Excursion into the Grotesque

I   Divertimento No. VII: Die Posaunen von Jericho
    (The Trumpets of Jericho)

DODERER wrote *Die Posaunen von Jericho* between the end of January and April 1951.[1] This last of his "Divertimenti" was written after he had ceased (for twenty-five years) to experiment with this form. Surprisingly, Doderer regarded this Divertimento as one of his most successful works, together with the novels *Die Wasserfälle von Slunj* and *Die Merowinger* (*ChiR*, 85).

In his essay "Bases and Function of the Novel," Doderer refers to "Trumpets" as an example of the "priority of form over content" (WdD, 163). He elaborates how the conception of this story suddenly came to him, primarily as a "clear and detailed dynamic image" (WdD, 163), which he quickly drew on his drafting board. His sketch outlines the four-movement form, assigns themes and three varying tempi to the four movements, the last movement being the longest and most important. The sequence of tempi—fresh, sustained, grotesque, smooth (cf. DW, 70)—parallels the sequence of movements in Classical symphonies, particularly if we substitute "scherzo" for "grotesque."

As René Tschirky has shown in his thorough analysis,[2] there exists a complicated and rich subtext in this story, and therefore a plot summary may be inadequate. But it may serve as a beginning.

Told in the first person, the story is set in the early 1950s, in the outskirts of Vienna. The narrator witnesses—or thinks he witnesses—a child's being molested by a man with an extraordinarily large nose. The presumed molester, named Rambausek, shortly thereafter approaches the narrator with a request to borrow a small amount of money to satisfy the blackmail demand made by the parents of the child. Instead of repayment, the narrator, who loathes Rambausek because of his large nose, requires Rambausek to perform three deep-knee bends on a busy sidewalk.

From their first encounter in a dark entryway, the narrator speaks with contempt of Rambausek's features, his subservient manner, and his low social standing. Yet as soon as Rambausek has performed the ridiculous deep-knee bends, the narrator beings to realize that his behavior was unnecessary and unjustified. Not surprisingly, the final sentence of the first movement indicates the narrator's reassessment of Rambausek, who has grown in moral stature above his own, particularly after he greets the narrator on the street "with great deference" (*ChiR*, 10). The deterioration of the narrator—the writer and artist—has begun, and after tracing his decline, the story tells of his slow healing, or perhaps rebirth.

In the second movement, the narrator takes long walks on the outskirts of the city, particularly along a river, where the wreck of a steamer protrudes from the water. Among the children playing near the wreck he seeks the little girl whom he thought he saw with Rambausek in the initial episode. She has a brief conversation with the narrator, long enough to establish that she knows who he is. For no particular reason, the narrator feels poisoned by melancholy or longing (*Wehmut*). The little girl is clearly associated with a distasteful episode; she even is said to have something revolting (*unappetitlich*) about her. The wreck of the steamer may be seen as a symbol for the narrator's own failures: "I stared fixedly at the demolished paddle-box of the steamer, as if I could read from these remains how matters stood in the fundamental plexus of my being" (*ChiR*, 12).

Throughout the story, metaphors of movement, or more particularly transportation, reflect the narrator's inner condition. Thus, while he contemplates the wreck of the steamer, he conjures visions of a train gliding down an incline after having traveled through two tunnels. The feeling of release and abandon, of gliding toward finality, occur not only in *Die Posaunen von Jericho* but also in "Begegnung im Morgengranen," where the protagonist finally accepts (albeit semi-consciously) the approach of his own death. The culmination of *Die Posaunen von Jericho* also includes the metaphor of an effortless glide along train tracks.

The third movement—the Scherzo—contains the most grotesque elements, and is in fact called the *Grotesksatz*. The narrator sinks deeper and deeper into drunkenness and senseless brawling, and his friends devise a prank to scare a gentle old lady who shares the large apartment of the narrator. A trio of trombones—the German biblical episode refers to trombones rather than trumpets—is hired to play after midnight in front of the rooms of the old lady. The trombones intone the "Triumphal March" from Verdi's *Aida,* and the friends

Excursion into the Grotesque

rush into the old lady's quarters firing toy pistols. The prank fails because the intended victim is not at home at the time. The horde is embarrassed, swiftly arrested by the police, arraigned, and given suspended sentences for gross mischief.

The last movement, the *Finalsatz*, begins with the narrator in the depths of depression. He is about to move temporarily into the apartment of a friend who is a painter, while the latter is away in Paris. The order and cleanliness of the studio shame the narrator deeply because they accent his own debauched behavior. But here he still feels haunted by Rambausek and all he associates with him. His walks again take him to the river and the wreck, and closer and closer to his old neighborhood.

He meets Rambausek and his wife, together with Mr. and Mrs. Jurak, parents of the little girl Rambausek had supposedly molested. The narrator is puzzled that, after the blackmail, the two couples go for walks together. But still more curiously, Mr. Jurak practically pushes his wife onto the narrator, and soon he finds himself sitting in a café, drinking wine, and lustfully squeezing and fondling Mrs. Jurak. The episode is repeated soon thereafter, but this time, in an embarrassing reversal, Rambausek sees the narrator and Mrs. Jurak together in the dark corner.

After the two leave the café to meet Mrs. Jurak's little daughter, the action suddenly quickens as the two approach the wreck where the girl has again been playing. She has fallen into the wreck and has been pulled out by Rambausek, who, having almost drowned, is lying unconscious on the sidewalk. During the rescue operations, the narrator watches Rambausek closely, concentrating again on his enormous nose. He now recalls an episode from his younger years when a passing gentleman with a full beard provoked his anger to the extent that he pulled the beard of the unsuspecting passer-by.

Sensing the relevance of this past event to the present situation, the narrator suddenly feels compelled to act in a similar manner. He rushes to Rambausek's side, grasps his nose and tugs at it vigorously. Rambausek is roused from his unconscious state and soon whisked away by an ambulance. The *Nasenriss* seems to have dissipated the narrator's feelings of anxiety, melancholy, and sterility. He returns to his work, and soon is on his way to "the West" to see about the publication of a major work. The final image, recurring here for about the fifth time, is that of a train gliding down an incline, after having struggled upward. Together with the rhythmical and effortless train motion, the colors green, blue, and gold predominate. The narrator's regained freedom is reflected in the remark: ". . . .What would we live for, if we weren't liberated at last in the final movement?" (E, 189).

Critics took their cue from Doderer's "Nineteen Curricula Vitae" in paying close attention to *Die Posaunen von Jericho*." Weber sees this story as Doderer's third attempt with the Divertimento form—not counting the six completed in the 1920s. The other two—*Das Geheimnis des Reiches* and *Das letzte Abenteuer*—failed because they grew beyond Doderer's own prescribed length: forty minutes or less of reading aloud. Weber points out that, although still slightly too long for a Divertimento, *Die Posaunen von Jericho* illustrates in an exemplary way the priority of form over content. The last movement successfully integrates themes from the preceding three, while the mood, tempo, and tone of each movement remain distinct. In the polycentric or mosaic technique and in the choice of title, Doderer looks back to *Die Strudlhofstiege* and *Die Dämonen* but also anticipates his uncompleted tetralogy *Roman No VII*.

Heinz Politzer stresses the a-logical, a-moral, a-psychological aspects of *Die Posaunen von Jericho*, arguing that the events portrayed are not interconnected, and while they are not impossible, "their common senselessness may be seen as the first element of their unity."[3] For example, the relationship between the *Nasenriss* and Rambausek's revival is at best incongruous. Politzer even goes so far as to say that it leans toward the literature of the Absurd.

The significance of the title seems clear to Politzer: "Jericho. . .is the soul of the narrator frozen in the frost of its own absurdity."[4] What is unclear is the precise nature of the "disease" from which the narrator seems to have been healed in the end. Politzer apparently underrated the introductory episode: The narrator does not see things clearly, and is therefore guilty of a cardinal sin in Doderer's moral universe: *Apperceptions-Verweigerung*, prejudices, unwarranted inferences and conclusions, in short, a cluttered perception of reality.

Politzer also stresses Doderer's radical break with the tradition of the *Dichterfürst*, the notion of the priestly posture and function of the poet, cultivated by, among others, Thomas Mann.[5] The narrator of *Die Posaunen von Jericho*, on the other hand, writes "during and in spite of his spiritual disease,"[6] and he has managed to get on with his work even at the time of what were to him disgusting excesses with Mrs. Jurak. Doderer chooses as narrator an almost ridiculous figure, whom Politzer likens to a "sad clown," existing at a lower

Excursion into the Grotesque

level than some of the figures to whom the narrator considers himself superior.

Michael Shaw's interpretation of *Die Posaunen* starts with the narrator's initial failure of perception, his hasty judgment, and dubious conclusions. The narrator has seen Rambausek's long nose, considers it obscene, and its owner *a fortiori* an obscene person who commits obscene acts. Shaw also notes that Mrs. Jurak's daughter is described as paralleling her mother's vulgar seductiveness. It is therefore conceivable that Rambausek has been manipulated all along, that he has, in fact, been led "by the nose" *and* victimized by Mrs. Rambausek, just as the narrator eventually is victimized by her.

Thus Shaw interprets the *Nasenriss* as a considerably more adequate and lighthearted way of dealing with a large nose than the elaborate accusations and condescending punishments which the narrator visits upon Rambausek. However scurrilous the action may seem, tugging at the nose dramatizes a philosophical position: it addresses a specific source of irritation or provocation, and does not lead to "the inveterate and deeply rooted tendency to 'account' for phenomena by reference to causes that allegedly give rise to them."[7]

The most detailed analysis of *Die Posaunen* has been undertaken by René Tschirky. Considering preliminary drafts, an earlier title (*Aus meinem Leben*), internal evidence, and Doderer's own statements in *Die Tangenten* and diaries, Tschirky thoroughly studies the careful composition and elaborate symbolic structure of *Die Posaunen*. He sees the main development of the story as beginning with a description of the narrator's confused mind, which does not respond adequately to people or events. Even the language used to describe his mind reveals his inadequacy through use of false elements and pseudometaphors. Only toward the end of the last movement does the language become clean and uncluttered again. Tschirky does not see *Die Posaunen* as an excursion into realms of the absurd—as does Politzer—or as a veiled statement on the inadequacy of language. In agreement with Michael Shaw, Tschirky considers *Die Posaunen* an illustration and restatement of one of Doderer's central concerns, which has as its center the problem of apperception, and the artist's direct and reliable grasp of reality.

Tschirky does emphasize that the freedom the narrator experiences after the crucial *Nasenriss*—a grotesquely funny *epiphany*—cannot be earned, but is "added" (*hinzugegeben*) only when the protagonist displays an inner readiness.

Tschirky adds an important observation concerning the trombone prank, which he sees as a perversion of the biblical model because here evil seeks to conquer good, and the sense of the Old Testament events turns into nonsense. The trombone episode is seen by Tschirky as a model of revolutionary behavior, of collective action in general, and of anti-Semitism in particular.[8] The actions of the gang of friends illustrate the manifestation of maniacal, monstrous, even demonic forces. They are, in Doderer's scholastic thinking, intrusions of *nihil* into the harmony of being. We may thus see the elements of the grotesque in *Die Posaunen* as representations of evil. This brief foray into grotesquery in *Die Posaunen* was to become a full-scale expedition in Doderer's novel *Die Merowinger oder Die totale Familie*.

II Holiday of a Realist

On March 1, 1951, while Doderer was working on the last movement of *Die Posaunen* as well as on *Die Dämonen*, he noted in his diary: "In *Die Merowinger* I'll create a reservation for the grotesque which otherwise does me mischief elsewhere."[9] Doderer's exuberant, slightly mischievous, often grotesque and acerbic imagination seems to have needed a safety valve. Nor is this a new development. Ever since "Die Peinigung der Lederbeutelchen" in the early 1930s, Doderer had written humorous works side by side with realistic ones. In a letter to Dietrich Weber, dated December 30, 1963, Doderer refers to *Die Merowinger* as the "holiday of a realist" (*Ferien eines Realisten*).[10] To be sure, writing to the same critic, Doderer also maintains that "everything grotesque points to the deep pessimism of its originator,"[11] so in approaching Doderer's grotesqueries one must remain conscious of two positions: works like *Die Merowinger* serve as an occasional escape from the discipline of realistic prose writing as well as revealing the dark, even tragic world view of their author. This apparent paradox cannot and must not be resolved. M. W. Swales writes: "It is. . .almost impossible to take [*Die Merowinger*] on any other level than that of a grotesque, enjoyable romp."[12] Herbert Eisenreich, on the other hand, considers *Die Merowinger* to be "tragedy in the mask of the eccentric" (*Tragik in der Maske des Kauzes*).[13] In a way, Doderer follows the footsteps of his great compatriot Johannes Nestroy, who combined with hilarious laughter a tragic view of life.

Die Merowinger represents the largest of Doderer's grotesqueries. Its main plot revolves around Childeric III, the last twentieth-century patriarch and descendant of the ancient Frankish dynasty of the Merovingians. He is a puny little man, who, through an outrageous sequence of marriages with widows of both his father and grandfather, has managed to become his own father, grandfather, stepson, and all the rest. In this manner, he has attempted to "totalize" the entire family within himself. The ludicrous outward symbol of this venture is his incredibly complicated beard, which is actually an accretion of the various beard styles of his forefathers. His dwarflike stature notwithstanding, he has been endowed with remarkable sexual prowess.

The most distinctive attribute of Childeric III, however, is his uncontrollably violent outbursts of anger. Doderer describes his *Wut* or *Grimm* as a "fundamental revolt" (*grundsätzliche Empörung*), as well as a form of atheism.[14] Other anger-prone protagonists are relegated to the class of cholerics, that is, mere psychological phenomena. Only Childeric III meets Doderer's requirements for true anger: "Only he who—in the moment of anger—wants nothing else in the world, except his own anger, is truly angry. . . . Anger is acute refusal to apperceive, panicked flight from life, a strange form of suicide where instead of killing himself one wants to kill all others. He wants there to be no life."[15]

After family conflicts have led to mock-heroic warfare, described in mock-tragic dialogue in the style of the Neo-Classicists, Childeric's machinations are finally stopped by castration. His enemies surprise him at night, cut his hair, shave his beards, and "un-man" him. Even after the "castrative problem solving" (*kastrative Problemlösung*) (MER, 362), Childeric continues to suffer from outbursts of uncontrollable anger. Periodically he boxes the ears of Mrs. Eygener, a quiet neighbor who soon adjusts both to the violence and to the "pain money" (*Schmerzensgeld*) which Childeric pays generously.

The main plot of Childeric's fate is surrounded by various stories, the most outrageously funny one being that of Dr. Horn, a psychiatrist-neurologist, who has devised a combination of ridiculously effective/ineffective therapies for his anger-stricken clients. In one therapy session, his nurse, Helga, marches the patients around the room while hammering their heads with drumsticks. Dr. Horn is a savage caricature of the sly, opportunistic doctor who knows how to balance the illusion of cure with the need for continued therapy. Various competitors, though, lure away Dr. Horn's business, one particular group specializing in anger therapy by pouch lancing: variously labeled, bead-filled pouches are punctured by the patients, who feel an immediate reduction of anger vis-à-vis the particular target represented by the pouch. There also exists a mysterious international organization, Hulesch & Quenzel, which specializes in provoking anger. Its agents may leave soot in a target's pocket, provide razor-sharp shirt buttons, or install a faucet in the middle of a sink. The activities of this organization belong to the "enjoyable romp" Swales speaks of.

An interesting figure is that of the narrator, Dr. Döblinger, in whom Doderer caricatures himself. Initially slightly impoverished, he is readily willing to profiteer from Dr. Horn's dubious operations. Döblinger is beaten several times, once with the expressed purpose of allaying the anger of the reader of the novel, who—Doderer assures us—must surely be angry with Dr. Döblinger for his outrageous tales. In an "Epilogue," Dr. Döblinger "explains" that the entire narrative has been nothing but nonsense (*Mordsblödsinn, Blödsinn, Unsinn*), an assertion we may or may not believe.

One additional figure needs to be mentioned: Pelimbert the Undiscussable (*der Indiskutable*). Even though he remains in the background, he, like the anger, seems to incorporate an aspect of Doderer's own character. Pelimbert has chosen a form of marginal adjustment; he remains passive, refuses to commit or engage himself, and in his radical nonparticipation has reached a detachment of Oriental proportions:

In the deepest roots of his thinking it was clear to Pelimbert. . .that the time at hand. . .had reached a degree of ridiculousness to which a man, whom blind fate had given the necessary means of survival, could only respond by refraining from any activity whatsoever; thereby not increasing a ridiculousness which was already undignified and repulsive. . . . Therefore it was important to throw everyone out in time, to remain in a relaxed attitude on the sofa or behind the empty desk, to place the bottle next to or on this, and to remain this way, as it were with Mission Zero. We are discretely charged with this Mission today, if we get to eat without having to fuss and kick [*strampeln*]. That's how Pelimbert thought, and he did not consider himself a nihilist, but rather a guardian [*Bewahrer*] who thought to have accomplished enough by refusing to contribute to the general corrosive ridiculousness [*alles zerfressende Lächerlichkeit*]. (MER, 116 - 17)

It would not be an exaggeration to conclude that Pelimbert illustrates or incarnates attitudes that Doderer shared for much of his life. Since the 1920s, particularly since his encounter with Gütersloh, he sought to stay out of the success-oriented, slick, production and publicity market of the literary world. The posture of the outsider who keeps a sharp eye on events but does not have the confidence to change them is shared by Pelimbert and Doderer.

Die Merowinger contains a perplexing mixture of humor and seriousness, and thus belongs to the genre of "tragicomedy." Pelimbert is a spiritual cousin to Dürrenmatt's Romulus the Great. Doderer's delightfully exuberant language establishes the novel as a superb grotesquery to which he has added a venomous persiflage of aspects of both totalitarian and modern society in general. Doderer adds the seriousness in subtle and even surreptitious ways, and one can therefore read through passages such as the one cited above without deep philosophizing. However, wider knowledge of Doderer's work and life adds a more significant dimension to *Die Merowinger*.

III Short and Shortest Grotesqueries

In the spirit of Doderer's flights of imagination, we must consider the Vignettes or very short stories from the 1950s and 1960s. Some, such as "Ehrfurcht vor dem Alter," are only a sentence long; nevertheless, they usually follow the same pattern of action. In "Ehrfurcht vor dem Alter" an old lady fusses at a post-office window. The narrator's anger is provoked to such an extent that he grasps an iron-clad club—"which he customarily carried with him for just such purposes" (E, 310)—to demolish the front of the house across the street. However, honoring old age, he feels prevented from direct intervention (*Ausschreitung*). Usually, in Doderer's writing, anger provokes an intensity of emotion which he then translates into ludicrously enormous gestures; and, frequently, objects seem to contain a certain maliciousness (*Tücke des Objekts*), and thus the reaction of a protagonist may even include the "punishment" of objects.

At other times, grotesque creatures seem to be direct representations of evil. Related to Kafka's Odradek, Doderer's *Peinigl* is such a manifestation of unprovoked hostility. Doderer describes the *Peinigl* as a vicious little catlike creature, whose function is to provoke anger and hostility. Once a *Peinigl* infests a human community, the life of the inhabitants is guaranteed to be filled with "poison, gall and mutual hostility" (E, 321). One aspect of this evil infestation is its accidental beginning. Anger, or evil, so Doderer seems to say, is inherent in human nature, and strikes at random.

In a short story entitled "Trethofen," which might best be translated as "Kicksville," Doderer makes light of the customs of civilized human communication: social interaction seems based on convention rather than on universally valid metaphysical laws. In

"Trethofen" the narrator arrives in a little village by that name and soon observes with some astonishment that members of this community interact—among other ways—by means of vigorously applied kicks in the rear, usually without interrupting the flow of their conversation. The host at the inn is unable to articulate a satisfactory answer to the repeated inquiries of the narrator concerning these strange customs. But in the end the narrator reveals a degree of commonality of spirit by dumping a bucket of whitewash over a group of men engaged in conversation and kicks. In his nevertheless hasty departure—*Nicht versagte mein Starter*—he muses, not without admiration, that there is something fascinating about "the ways of the troglodyte" (E, 332), especially since he senses incipient tendencies to such a way of life within himself.

The spirit of scurrilous satire permeates Doderer's writings from the beginning, although the realism of his major works tends to distract from the grotesque humor. In his *Repertorium* Doderer noted: "In art there is no border separating seriousness and humor. If both are perfectly expressed they can continuously shuttle back and forth between each other. They belong to the same level: Voices in the sweet play, different segments of the orchestral palette, like strings or wind instruments. Nothing else" (Rep, 208). Strict separation of genres, as well as closely observed levels of style, do not seem consonant with Doderer's poetics. While there is a great deal of outright tomfoolery in some of his works, in a sense he does take his humor seriously.

CHAPTER 6

The Late Phase: facta loquuntur

I *"Basis and Function of the Novel"*

THE volume *Wiederkehr der Drachen* (Return of the Dragons) contains most of Doderer's major essays, treatises, and speeches. As the bibliography to the present volume indicates, however, Doderer's theoretical writings number over 200 items, dating from 1921 to the last year of his life. In the beginning, many of his newspaper articles were published under pseudonyms or anonymously, and some are undoubtedly lost. Nevertheless, together with *Tangenten, Repertorium, Commentarii 1951 - 1956,* the unpublished diaries, "Nightbooks," and sketches, they constitute a kind of tool box of Doderer's ideas. Here he could not only develop his reflections on poets, poetics, aesthetics, religion, and philosophy, but could also satisfy his need to separate theories about writing from his novels. To be sure, sometimes, as in the case of *Die Strudlhofstiege,* the beginning of a novel would be found in diary entries. But by and large, Doderer kept his serious philosophizing apart from his fiction. That does not mean that he developed a system of aesthetics or philosophy. Neither does it mean that reflection is absent from his novels. Rather, his reflective writings constitute a kind of dialogue with himself. Phrases tend to recur, and exhortations to himself may be repeated again and again, sometimes with the monotony of a prayer and sometimes with its intensity.

The constant probing of the relationship between life and writing preoccupied Doderer all his life. Reduced to a simple scholastic formula—a Doderer penchant—the alternative seems to him to be *vivere deinde scribere* or *scribere deinde vivere.* In the end, it became clear to Doderer that it was writing that taught him to live, or at any rate that was primary. In an interview with Jośe A. Palma Caetano, his Portuguese translator, Doderer replied to the question why had he become a writer and what literature meant to him: "I became a writer [*Schriftsteller*] because I felt that in this way I could deal with life [*mit dem Leben fertig werden*]. . ." (Erinn, 33).

This must not be understood to mean that Doderer withdrew into realms of his own imagination, thus avoiding contact with the difficulties and problems of the real world. Neither does it indicate that Doderer saw his role as that of a positivist, collecting details of life in seemingly random inclusiveness. Doderer occupies a position in the history of the modern novel which is difficult to specify because he worked in comparative isolation from modern trends. Weber accurately observes: "Doderer constitutes the exact middle between Naturalism, for which facts are everything, and Symbolism, for which facts are nothing, which is only concerned with their meaning" (DW, 217).

Doderer has repeatedly stated the center of his theory of the novel, perhaps most succinctly in the above-mentioned interview: "By the way, many things are called novels which aren't. For example there is no novel *about* something; that's nonsense! A novel is always about life·that is around us, built of the trivial material that surrounds us, and it makes this material translucent and suspends it, or: the novel breaks windows into existing walls, we look out through these windows. That is the function of the novel" (Erinn, 34).

The function of the novel, according to Doderer, thus lies beyond the novel itself. It is a means to make us see an extraliterary reality. Or alternately: "Openness to the totality of the world is the aesthetic premise of [Doderer's] novels."[1] It is not surprising that the most frequent metaphor in Doderer's writing is that of openness. Again and again, characters in his fiction look through windows, and either they are able to see, or they fail this simple but crucial test. Thus Geyrenhoff, the narrator of *Die Dämonen*, has a splendid view from his atelier, while Donald Clayton, in *Die Wasserfälle von Slunj*, is horrified and in a sense blinded by the wall of water that his window during a rainstorm represents to him. The ability to see out through a window may be an indication of the spiritual health of a Doderer character.

In this context we can perhaps understand Doderer's preoccupation in the last phase of his writing with what he called either *roman muet* or *stummer Roman*, that is, the "mute novel." Again, in the interview with Palma Caetano, Doderer defined his conception of the mute novel: "No statements, no words of the poet, no sententiae, no marginal notes, nothing of all that! But shape, shaping of life! [*Aber Gestalt—Gestaltung des Lebens!*]" (Erinn, 36). His goal, then, seems to have been the novel as still life, mute because it selects apparently trivial objects. The interpretation of what is shown—and this is a crucial compositional principle of Doderer's later novels—must be added by the viewer or reader. It is in that sense that "the facts speak." In Doderer's diaries the phrase *facta loquuntur* recurs frequently.

The most detailed statement of Doderer's theory of the novel is found in his essay "Bases and Function of the Novel" (1959). In it he proceeds from the assumption or observation that the modern—perhaps postmedieval—world tends to disintegrate pluralistically, and that the novel can and should reintegrate the world. The novel is thereby claiming universality, and in the end "giving us renewed joy of life [*eine neue Lust zu leben*]" (WdD, 149 - 50). As indicated earlier, the novelist must live and work with the paradox of having as an object of representation the world, while the demands of his art force limitation and selection. Doderer sees the only approximate solution to this contradiction as an attempt at "objective representation" (WdD, 154).

In the second part of "Bases and Function," a speech given at the *Société des Études Germaniques* in Paris in 1958, Doderer elaborates on the crucial importance of memory for the attitude of the "epic writer," a term he uses consistently and intentionally. The essential aspect of memory lies, according to him in its nonvoluntary, or prerational, selectivity. In a position close to that offered by the manifestos of Surrealism, Doderer maintains that memory in a sense takes care of "choosing between the significant and the insignificant" (WdD, 158). In the final analysis, he seems convinced that "the innermost core of narrative prose. . .is thoroughly poetic, that this prose has a similar *punctum nascendi* as every poem: a nonrational one. Underneath narrative prose the epic verse is still cryptically cascading [*rauscht heute noch kryptisch der epische Vers*]" (WdD, 159).

To keep his finely tuned memory active, the novelist must in a sense disregard himself, must resist the temptation to complete or perfect himself: "He is someone who wants neither to work on the world, nor on himself, truly someone without goals" (WdD, 160). Doderer, whose theoretical writings abound with vivid images, compares the novelist to someone sitting halfway up a tree looking along a perplexing multitude of branches, none of which he is permitted to climb. Only the saint may climb upward along the trunk, "leaving behind the novelist in the confusion of branches, branchlets and twigs, the last man who will defend the complexity and wholeness of life to the extreme, against any final solution. . ." (WdD, 161). We can see how political undertones color Doderer's thoroughly antiideological aesthetics.

The universality that comes with objective representation, with resistance to "solutions," that comes also from deep moral convictions, also necessitates wide learning on the part of the novelist. One of his main attributes has to be accessibility (*Zugänglichkeit*). His epistemology is a simple one in that he trusts the surface reality: "[The novelist] begins by intensely embracing the knowability of the created world, based on what it shows in its changing flow. And he holds the firm opinion that phenomena as they present themselves are what they seem to be. . . . One could call the novelist an individual who has in him a distant reflection of the *analogia entis*. . . . One might be tempted to call him something like a born Thomist" (WdD, 166 - 67). Here we find the Christian core of Doderer's aesthetics: being partakes of the Divine.

Lest it be thought that Doderer is a positivist realist in Thomist disguise, it must be stressed that he is fully aware of the dual aspect of language as a tool for the creative imagination and a tool for analysis. As he points out, for his work the novelist must use "material" (language) in such a way that it fulfills both functions, in Doderer's terms *gestaltweis* and *zerlegungsweis*, that is, to shape or form and to analyze (cf. WdD, 168). Neither function must predominate. Doderer resorts to the image of two synchronized pistons; after the *Gestaltung* piston has pushed forward, the analytical foray will follow, which in turn leads to pure descriptiveness, and so forth. In spite of the unsubtle image, the dual aspect of language seems clear in Doderer, and his novels amply illustrate both analysis and description.

II Roman No 7/I: Die Wasserfälle von Slunj
(*The Waterfalls of Slunj*)

Doderer's last, unfinished writing project was the so-called *Roman No VII* (Novel Number Seven), envisioned by him as a sequence of four novels. Doderer finished the first, *Die Wasserfälle von Slunj* (1963, Engl. transl., 1966), as well as substantial portions of the second, *Der Grenzwald* (The Forest at the Border, publ. 1967). We have only sketchy knowledge of Doderer's vision of this massive composition. In the Palma-Caetano interview Doderer hinted at a symphonic four-movement composition, the intended similarity between the first and fourth novel—which were to be "loosened and light" (*aufgelockert und leicht*)—and the two middle novels were to exemplify Doderer's idea of the *roman muet*. With characteristic hyperbole Doderer concluded the interview by saying: "No one will be able to prove that I said something—I said nothing at all! I have used language like the sculptor uses clay and the painter uses color, nothing else" (Erinn, 37 - 38). To be sure, Doderer was thinking of *Der Grenzwald* when making the last statement.

Die Wasserfälle von Slunj weaves interrelated, or at least contiguous, strands of narrative around the fate of the two protagonists, father Robert and son Donald Clayton, British industrialists with a branch factory in Vienna. The parent-child motif pervades the novel in varying guises. The strength and spontaneity of the father, and the comparative weakness and awkwardness of the son, and thus the theme of decline, places this novel close to other family chronicles, such as Thomas Mann's *Buddenbrooks*, or Galsworthy's *Forsyte Saga*.

On first reading, the novel may seem to be loosely composed. Contributing to this looseness is the subdivision into approximately 140 short sections. But it soon becomes clear that the various episodes are linked to one another. As Weber has pointed out, Doderer follows the principle of "composed non-composition" (*komponierte Kompositionslosigkeit*), which may give the appearance of abruptness, in that new episodes are begun again and again.[2] But the appearance of decentralization does not obscure the clear, balanced story, and the closely woven texture of symbols and symbolic actions. Doderer treats the epicenters of the action with great care and seriousness. He takes considerable pains in describing how the two prostitutes, Finy and Fevrl, play with their toes while sunbathing, and he establishes that surface trivia are as much part of the reality of his novel as the deep fears haunting Donald Clayton.

The sequence of two generations, and, in part, their conflict, is most clearly personified by the two Claytons. Donald is conceived on the evening of his parents' honeymoon visit to the waterfalls of Slunj, in Croatia. Born in Vienna in 1878, he is brought to England when he has reached school age. There he lives in the house of his grandfather, a venerable, punctual, and exacting Briton who takes great interest in his grandson's learning. Compared to the demands of the public school, the demands of Donald's grandfather are very high. Donald, therefore, excels in school. Growing up with German, English, and several other languages, Donald studies engineering in Vienna and graduates from the Technical University in 1902. Thereafter he works in the Vienna factory of Clayton & Powers.

Outwardly, father and son Clayton look so much alike that they are known as the Clayton brothers. One phrenological detail clearly distinguishes them from one another: the son has inherited the mother's skull shape, which is flattened at the back, but Robert Clayton's head is rounded. The woman for whose love father and son compete notices the difference. The rounded head seems to be Doderer's formula for apperceptiveness, and, considering the location of the occipital lobe, this detail may be well chosen. Be that as it may, Donald lacks accuracy and spontaneity of perception and reaction. Together with a certain exterior awkwardness and stiffness, he possesses a highly controlled, almost too thoughtful manner. A thoroughly kind and considerate person, he does not seem to be able to form strong attachments, remaining—as Doderer repeatedly calls it—*unbeteiligt* (not taking part).[3]

Unbeteiligt is part of his signature as a character and is not accurately translated by either "aloof" or "unconcerned," as in the existing translation. Perhaps Donald's "impartial" attitude is best illustrated in an incident during his school years in England. At his grandfather's house, his nursemaid, Kate Thürriegl, and the housekeeper, Mrs. Cheef, compete for Donald's affection and loyalty. At one time they are engaged in a loud dispute about their authority over the young master during the grandfather's absence. Their verbal battle is stopped short by Donald, who sticks his head out of the door of his room and calmly and "impartially" announces: "Please stop that noise" (WoS, 135). Unconcerned with what is being discussed, Donald simply wishes that there should be no noise.

Whereas Donald is an excellent engineer, a polite and considerate son, and a close friend at least to the deputy director Chwostik, he is also haunted by subrational fears and nightmares, originating, Doderer suggests, during prenatal life and very early childhood. As Franz P. Haberl has pointed out in his investigation of the water imagery in Doderer's novels, water seems to Donald either stagnant, or like an enclosing, stifling wall.[4] One of Donald's recurring nightmares focuses on the terror brought on by falling masses of water. Either he imagines the horizontal surface of a lake having tilted to become a vertical wall of water, or he sees the view through a window obscured by rain, yielding the impression of being walled in by water. The presence of such an elemental force paralyzes Donald. He feels imprisoned and has the desire to look at where the masses of water have hit the ground, yet he finds himself unable to do so. Doderer suggests at one point that if Donald had had the strength to get up and look through the window, he would have dispelled his fears, seeing that the dreaded wall of water was merely rain "that did no damage to the garden" (WoS, 126).

But Donald cannot rid himself of his peculiar paralysis. The most fateful incident of his inaction occurs one evening when he is with Monica Bachler, an intelligent, desirable woman whom Donald loves. Not without experience in matters of sex, Donald nevertheless simply does not react to her unmistakable desire to sleep with him. His cautiousness, considerateness, and deep-seated fears work together to keep him from simple and natural interaction. As Monica waits for him, undressed in bed, he sits in an adjoining room, politely waiting for an even clearer invitation. At this point, his inaction is transformed into paralysis by a sudden rain, because the fear of being walled in by water immobilizes him. An irretrievable opportunity is missed. Donald loses Monica, who will eventually marry Robert Clayton, by that time a widower for several years.

Several parallel and contrasting episodes are grouped around Donald's most serious failure. The most direct contrast is represented by the one evening that Monica and Chwostik spend together. Chwostik quite literally embraces the moment. Monica and Chwostik's evening also is surrounded by water imagery, but in this case, the waters are flowing, part of the force of life and Eros.

Another contrasting episode involves the pupil (*Gymnasiast*) Zdenko von Chlamtatsch, who responds to seduction by an older woman with unmistakable—and thoughtless—assent. The incident takes place in the bedroom of Monica, who is kind enough to lend her older lady friend her apartment for this occasion.

Zdenko, who, with some of his friends, emulates the British way of life represented to him by the Claytons, is also an antagonist to Donald. He delivers—unintentionally, it seems—the news to Donald that Monica has been seeing his father. Zdenko then happens to see Donald losing his balance, then recovering it with a "whirling and lanky motion" (*mit einer ausfahrenden und langstieligen Bewegung*) (WvS, 284). At the end of the novel, Zdenko again observes Donald making the same awkward gesture, occurring at the very moment of his death. Donald dies of fright and his body falls onto a precipice just under the edge of waterfalls of Slunj.

Doderer underscores in very small details the lack of ease from which Donald suffers. Both father and son smoke pipes. But the father holds his pipe dangling down in a relaxed manner, whereas Donald's pipe sticks out straight. Thus Doderer indicates, in a way that can easily be overlooked, that Donald bites down on his pipe stem. The term *verbissen* is clearly suggested.

The most important figure, next to the Clayton family, is Chwostik, a parallel figure to Leonhard Kakabsa, familiar from *Die Dämonen*. Chwostik works his way up from a job dealing in religious articles, to become Deputy Director (*Prokurist*) of the Clayton & Powers factory in Vienna. The loving portrayal of this ordinary-extraordinary character is a typical challenge to Doderer. As a narrator, he approaches Chwostik with a combination of love and understanding. Chwostik has a kind of sour contenance. Doderer refers to him repeatedly as *säuerlich*—and eventually Chwostik is assigned the not exactly complimentary epithet of *Runzel*, someone gnarled, wrinkled, and gnomish. Sometimes though the term is altered to the "affectionate" form, *Rünzelchen!* (little wrinkle-man).

Chwostik has the all-important quality of being accessible (*zugänglich*), apperceptive, and able to act and react spontaneously and accurately. He has an active memory but he is also able to live entirely in the present. A motif that is associated with him combines aspects of flowing time with time standing still. Thus, during the evening with Monica, we read of a "floating island. . .on the great river of time" (WoS, 243). And after Chwostik has moved into an apartment near the Prater, he stands at his window gazing out: "In those minutes, while he lingered at the window, gazing across the Prater, the disk of time began to revolve more swiftly under him, while he himself hovered above it, motionless as certain insects in the meadows, and in a void that he had never felt before, young as he was" (WoS, 110). At that moment, Chwostik experiences in a strangely intense way the past and the future. "He pictured the future. . .with the revolving of that disk, year after year sameness would be piled upon sameness, in thin strata as of ash, like dust upon dust. For the fraction of an instant all the everydayness of things, all that recurred as a matter of course with every dawning day lay upon him with all the weight of an immense effort that—far from gliding past unheeded—had to be accomplished afresh every time and in every detail" (WoS, 110 - 11).

Chwostik moves with ease and success in the world of business, leads the charmed life of one who is liked by everyone, learns fast—including an incredible array of languages—and moves without awkwardness. Yet he is not simply a well adjusted robot, but also a sensitive, yet limited man, who experiences fear, without being overwhelmed by it, who is touched by auras, or smells, and who is open to varieties of moods and mysteries. Yet Chwostik is a relatively lonely man. His parents have been dead for some time, and though he remembers scenes from his childhood vividly, especially his feeling of not having had enough room, he does not interact with the older generation.

The theme of the sequence of generations is treated more extensively in conjunction with several subsidiary characters. Andreas Milohnić, Chwostik's friend and "advisor" and man of all seasons to the Clayton family, is shown in a cordial relationship with his father, the captain of the steamer presently crossing Lake Constance.

Not so harmonious is the relationship between the *Hausmeisterin* Wewerka and her stepson Münsterer. The mother's goal is vicious and stifling dominance. But Münsterer manages to escape, improves himself, and becomes a satisfied Postal Director in Hungary. There is also the calculating Paul Harbach who, against his father's wishes (and supported by a rich countess), decides to study medicine in Munich. Paul's departure is cool and extremely rational. He remains aloof, and even at the occasion of his *engagement* he remains an "outsider": "He was completely convinced that he was doing the absolutely right thing. Outsiders always do the right thing" (WoS, 334).

The relationship between Monica and her parents is similarly distant. Monica is actually an illegitimate child. She pursues the profession of an engineer, uncommon for a woman at the beginning of the century. But she is serious and successful in establishing her independence. She does not, however, take her parents seriously and is reduced to laughter when Robert Clayton intimates that he would ask her father for permission to marry her.

There seems to be no clear direction in the sequence of generations, and surely no clear indication of decline. Only in the case of the Clayton family is the father visibly healthier and stronger than the son. Other children either rebel, become independent, ignore their parents, or, like Chwostik and Milohnić, rise socially above the positions of their parents. The final impression is one of criss-crossing lines of development, a complicated texture of individual fates selected from all levels of society.

Among the motifs of *Die Wasserfälle von Slunj*, the one most significant for its composition is that of the return, sometimes modified to recurrence or parallelism. Thus Donald returns to the place where he was conceived, and Chwostik, after thirty-some years, makes a nocturnal visit to his old apartment. Harriet Clayton keeps returning to England, to her favorite room in her uncle's estate, Pompe House. It happens to be a small, brown-paneled room that represents security and happiness for Donald's mother. For her son the experience of a walled-in existence will become much more ominous. For Finy and Feverl, the two affectionately portrayed prostitutes, the return to childhood country life represents fulfillment.

For Robert Clayton, the repetition of episodes after thirty or more years becomes highly significant. When he is on his honeymoon with Harriet, they travel along the Semmering, where the railroad crosses a viaduct—a huge railroad bridge. Robert is inexplicably impressed with the grandeur of the countryside and this stunning masterpiece of bridge building. He dashes from one window to another like an excited boy, while Harriet languidly remains in her compartment. After Harriet's death and Robert meets Monica, he will remember the railroad journey. It so happens that Monica made the same journey, and she reponds with enthusiasm to his description, and the evocation of grandeur and awe, combined with the disinterested glance of the engineer. Doderer describes Monica's and Robert's first conversation as a "duet." Their instinctive sharing of each other's sensibility is the beginning of their love.

The backward movement of memory through time is also linked to the motif of the crayfish (*Krebs*). Again, Doderer constructs paralleled situations contrasting Harriet and Monica. When Robert Clayton and Harriet first arrived in Slunj during their honeymoon, they had eaten deliciously prepared crayfish and had subsequently decided to see where these crustaceans lived. Having arrived at the pond, Robert at once lies down flat on his belly and soon catches a specimen. Harriet stays far back in the meadow, only approaching reluctantly. Thirty-some years later, Robert and Monica find themselves in a parallel situation, with a marked difference. At a garden party, where the host keeps crayfish in a pond, both Monica and Robert kneel at the edge of the pond and catch crayfish by hand, playfully comparing the sizes of their catch. This time it is Robert's son Donald who stands passively nearby. In Doderer's repertoire of symbolic actions, this "hunt" unmistakably indicates the closeness of Monica and Robert, the similarity of their approach to life, and the fact that they seem destined for each other.

The motif of the crayfish pervades all of Doderer's works, beginning as early as *Die Bresche*. Several aspects of this motif seem important: the primitive, retrograde motion, the fearful and strange appearance, and the curious stalking dignity of the animal. Describing its armor and the fierceness of its claws, Doderer links the crayfish motif with his notion of the dragon.[5] Like a leftover from another age, the crayfish seems linked with notions of conservativeness. It appears armored like a knight from the deep, and it is long-lived, because it has few natural enemies.

Aside from the positive associations, there is also something terrifying about these animals. To Harriet they appear like spiders, and Doderer repeats an image he first used in *Die Bresche:* the whip of a circus director compared to the antennae of a giant crayfish. The suggested implication is horrid.

An additional aspect of Robert Clayton's crayfish hunt needs to be underscored: Robert, who has had no experience in catching crayfish, instinctively knows how and where to hold the animal so that it cannot harm him. It seems that Doderer means to signify that Robert lacks the fear to grasp at what may seem horrifying to some, and that his natural curiosity drives him to explore. Seen from this viewpoint, the motif of the crayfish becomes linked with the fear of primitive instinctual life, and the ability or willingness to handle the animals, at least in *Die Wasserfälle,* appears to be an indicator of control over one's fate. Characters in the novel who catch crayfish, or take an interest in them—like Chwostik—do not suffer paralyzing fears. Reaching out spontaneously to the unknown and accepting the risk seems to nullify dread.

The central symbol of the novel is without doubt the gigantic thundering mass of water that gives it its title and combines aspects of terror and destructiveness with aspects of beneficence. To the older Clayton, the sheer enormity of the vertical masses of roaring water seems like a lake or an ocean surface turned sideways. Typically, his view is dispassionate and analytical, although he is also touched by fear. A particular curiosity of the falls, which Doderer clearly made a part of his central symbol, are the bridges, huts, and mills which have been constructed at the very edge of the falls. The peasants who own the mills negotiate the slippery paths and pursue their dangerous work with sureness, routine, and probably without much thought. Robert and Harriet Clayton are strangely moved by the sight: "High up on the white-foaming edge—the lower part of the falls was lost in veils of spray—there were baffling details: little roofs, fences or the like, all made of old brown wood. It was those things up there that caused the sense of terror; they were really the most terrifying thing about the cataract, and yet it was utterly beyond the power of words to say why this was so" (WoS, 14).

Generally, water imagery represents "an elemental, primordial force,"[6] which may be life-giving or destructive, but it is neither good nor bad. Two particular aspects of the waterfalls, however, seem to have been overlooked by critics: their awesome and destructive nature *and* their function as a source of power for the peasants. Perhaps it is the numinous aspect of the waterfalls which represent the terror and grandeur of nature that was most important to Doderer. Doderer seems to say that elemental forces simply exist; they are a-moral, a-human, part of the way things are, and perhaps—at least for the milling peasants—useful. The terror of the falls is balanced by the wonder of their force. But our way of reacting, our success in integrating the presence of the "falls" into our life varies. The particular variation seems to be an accident of fate. Thus Donald Clayton does not become guilty and is therefore punished. Donald's mode of life is simply his own, in part inherited, and it just does not equip him for integrating the overwhelming and perhaps fierce aspects of life into his being. He is born too weak. For this reason he perishes when he is at the top of the falls, precisely where the peasants routinely mill their grain.

Seen as a whole, *Die Wasserfälle von Slunj* is a closely woven texture of symbols, knitted more closely, yet more translucently than most of Doderer's earlier novels. Most of the clusters of symbols center around familiar themes: apperceptiveness, memory, the ineluctable nature of personal fate, the joy and the tragedy of life. Doderer demonstrates these themes with little philosophizing and with a modicum of sententiousness on the part of the narrator. The characters' apperceptions, their memories, and their interactions, are in a sense portrayed superficially. That is, we see their actions and are not provided with lengthy or deep explanations. Doderer's is not a psychological novel. There is much left unsaid about his characters.

It is, of course, precisely Doderer's contention that reality is contained in the surface of things, and that what he calls the typically German (as distinct from Austrian) transreal novel is a failure. At one point in *Die Wasserfälle,* Doderer waxes declamatory while explaining Robert Clayton's ability to enjoy the surface of life, be it a train ride along a magnificent landscape, or the playful hunt of crayfish. Robert Clayton, so Doderer maintains, has mastered the art of living, because he has "exercised" this ability, and, Doderer adds apodictically: "Because this world is entirely contained in its lovely [*hold*] surface, and with all its 'depths' (especially with them); and anyone who doesn't want to believe that, may it please him to ask a painter" (WvS, 311).

In his "Commentari XVI" Doderer declared: "The view from the apperceptive reader into de-perceptive existence: that is Novel

Number Seven."[7] Translating his customary and laconic philosophical shorthand, we gather that Doderer intended the reader to view the novellistic world from a superior vantage point. (The narrator of *Die Wasserfälle* frequently assists in lifting the reader to such a superior position, demonstrating at the same time his own superiority.) The attentive reader may see relationships, intrusions of fate or accident, parallels or coincidences, to which the participants in the novel are blind. This blindness, or better, limitedness, of the figures in his novels, is seen by Lutz Werner Wolff as evidence of Doderer's "monadic" world view.[8] That is, the perceptions, and thus the interaction and communication of individual figures populating his novels are limited by their particular positions. Between the individual monads there is a void, rarely traversed. One instance of bridging the gap is Robert and Monica's "duet," the content of which is characteristically trivial, superficial, and surely accidental. The perhaps simple point is that the characters are portrayed as limited and less aware than either the narrator, or presumably the reader. Once more, if we take Doderer's sentenious remark seriously, we see that he perceived the function of the novel as making the reader see, making his audience apperceptive, and thus, in the final analysis, helping the reader to master life.

III   Roman No 7/II: Der Grenzwald *(The Forest at the Border)*

Doderer's last novel fragment, the second of a planned tetralogy, was published posthumously in 1967.[9] What knowledge we have of the overall design of the four-novel composition stems from the Palma-Caetano interview, diary entries, personal statements, and internal evidence. We know that in the two middle novels, Doderer intended to illustrate his concept of the *roman muet*. It is clear that in such a novel, the presence of the narrator was to be considerably more restrained than in *Die Wasserfälle von Slunj*, or for that matter in *Die Strudlhofstiege* or *Die Dämonen*. Emphasis was to be placed on objective representation. Doderer even spoke of *Eros zum Objectiven*, which was to be one of his guiding principles in the composition of *Der Grenzwald*. We also know from Ivar Ivask that "on a symbolic level in each of the parts or novels a different element was to predominate: water, earth, air and fire."[10] And it does seem clear enough that water symbolism pervades the first novel, *Die Wasserfälle von Slunj*.

In *Der Grenzwald* the symbolism of earth finds its way into the novel through the expanse of the Siberian-Eurasian landmass. The most important protagonists share the fate of prisoners of war, during and after the first World War, even though some live in relative freedom and isolation, and even though all live in relatively civilized comfort. Earth, symbolized by the Asian continent, seems to refuse to give up its prisoners—more so than any physical restraint associated with camp security. In one instance, a train of prisoners slowly makes its way toward the West, even crosses the Ural mountains, only to be turned back to Siberia in the end. The immensity of the land also serves to distort the sense of accurately subdivided sequential time. The prisoners slowly begin to live with the impression that they have been travelling forever.

Der Grenzwald is linked not only to *Die Wasserfälle*, but also to Doderer's early novel *Das Geheimnis des Reiches*, where history and personal biography were joined into a kaleidoscopic, even slightly disjointed narrative. With *Der Grenzwald* Doderer resumes the autobiographical approach, though in a much more indirect or discreet manner. Instead of the ever-present alter ego René Stangeler, the narrator in *Der Grenzwald*, although present, remains in the background, and events and fates are described from the perspective of several main characters. Key events are even repeatedly portrayed from the perspective of several participants—almost in the cinematic style of *Rashomon*.

Several characters from *Die Wasserfälle*, who had appeared only at the periphery, are now pulled into the center of the narrative: Zdenko von Chlamtatsch (renamed Heinrich Zienhammer), Vincenz Vertruba, Fritz Hofmock, and even "Doderer." Curiously, an ugly old nighttable, which had contained some stolen money and was given by Chwostik to the *Hausmeisterin* Wenidoppler, mysteriously reappears in *Der Grenzwald*, having found its way from Vienna to the wilderness of Siberia.

But the points of contact between *Die Wasserfälle* and *Der Grenzwald* lie more in shared background—Vienna and Siberia; in similar constellations of fathers and sons—in *Grenzwald* father and son Ventruba parallel the Claytons; and in the continuation of symbolic motifs, such as the sense of openness or apperceptiveness, the sense of being walled in, and the blindness or *Abwesenheit* of a character.

The ten completed chapters of *Der Grenzwald* describe the backgrounds of several of the intended main characters, their connection with each other as well as with the novellistic center, a crime committed by Heinrich Zienhammer: the betrayal of nine Hungarian fellow officers, which leads to their execution. Although

The Late Phase: facta loquuntur

the central episodes are placed in the year 1919, Doderer reaches back in time to 1882 and beyond, and forward to the year 1921.

Establishing the multi-centered composition, Doderer begins at the periphery, as he did in *Die Dämonen* and in *Die Wasserfälle*. The first chapter describes in rapid and laconic style the return of Vincenz Ventruba from a prisoner-of-war camp in Italy, in August of 1919. Doderer describes his reintegration into the world of normalcy and industry—the Ventrubas have a shoe factory—which is slowly reasserting itself after the first World War. The father-son relationship of the Ventrubas is relaxed and positive. Theirs is a section of the sunny, successful life of the upper bourgeoisie. The Ventrubas desire to live in the present, and while they lack neither memory nor foresight, they are not plagued by guilt or uncertainty. The war has been a bothersome interlude to them, an excrescence from the body of normalcy.

One of the themes of the first chapter is that of return, with returning to the present and returning to the past consistently intersecting each other. Continuity is linked with memory, and in the last paragraph of the first chapter, Doderer evokes in a lyrical and symbolically charged passage several important themes and motifs:

With spring the old alleys began to exude scents. One almost thought one was on a narrow path of present time, stepping over deep caverns of scents from the past. . . . There was a kind of—translucence which permitted a glance deep down into former fragrances or mists, but one didn't see, one smelled. One smelled through the depths of time, and one immediately understood that it had to smell like that, and that one belonged. Those were the last pushes of Ventruba's return home. Time hollowed itself [*es höhlte sich die Zeit*], including the immediate past, and what he had experienced in Italy. . .collected itself back there in a wide basin, and in its depth it grew distant from today. In the end it was almost as if nothing had happened in the meantime. The water of time stood clear, layer upon layer, yes, decade upon decade, and one could almost have thought that one could look down to the bottom. (GW, 22)

As Lutz Werner Wolff has stated, the first chapter portrays the unity of human beings with their entire past and future.[11] This unity is expressed symbolically in the combination of the layers and the fluidity of the pool of water. The subrational process of memory selection is intimated by Doderer's use of the sense of smell. Smelling the scents and the aura of a place includes a totality and immediacy of perception which cannot in the same way be achieved by deliberation. The passage harkens back to Leonard Kakabsa's mystical experience, when he answers the imagined question, "What was I born for? To Smell?" with an unequivocal "Yes!"

The symbolic joining of water and time is characteristic of Doderer's repertoire of symbols. And the narrator's glance into the "water of time" with its indistinguishable "layers" expresses Doderer's philosophy on the functioning of memory: events, people, or places spontaneously emerge from memory if the author, or a character of his creation, reaches the proper altitude, becomes receptive, accessible, or apperceptive to his own past.

Thus memory informs the compositional technique of this, as of so many other novels by Doderer. The narrative begins at an apparently arbitrary point—August 1919—follows this strand for a while, only to begin again at another, earlier point. The continuous shuttling and shifting from one "layer of time" to another, and thus the repeated retracing and eventual merging of narrative strands establishes a complicated web of events and continguities which the reader perceives only gradually.

The technique is analytical, presuming that essential events are found in the past, rather than in events unfolded in chronological order. Doderer employs simultaneity and convergence, and underscores the importance of the narrator's selecting and sifting consciousness.

The second chapter begins in the year 1913 and introduces the thirty-year-old Dr. Alfons Halfon. We encounter him in an attitude of remembering, although in his case, the memory is a frantic and painful search for the circumstances of his mother's death. As is suggested early and confirmed later, he is the illegitimate son of the villain of the novel, Heinrich Zienhammer.

The relationship between Halfon and his father-in-name is very different from that between the young Ventruba and his father. Old Ephraim Halfon, a businessman and a fanatical student of the scriptures and the Talmud, is pictured as a dark-bearded, intense family tyrant, a "high priest of Baal" (GW, 29). Suggestions of sacrificial slaughter surround him.

The clinical picture of Dr. Halfon's mother reveals disturbing suggestions of "suicide through illness." The mother, Thamar Halfon, seems to have lost the will to live after giving birth to Alfons. The central symbol of the book—the forest at the border into another realm (death)—is first touched by Alfons's investigation into his mother's death. The attending physician has written down her last words: "I go between the little trees to the gate of unconsciousness [*Ohnmacht*]" (GW, 40). And the symbolic forest of transition from life to death pervades the entire *Grenzwald* fragment.

The sinister nature of Halfon's father is underscored by a comment of Eggenbrecher, who had painted a portrait of Thamar Halfon. The old painter relates that he could never paint in the presence of the older Halfon, that he was paralyzed by him. He calls him the "anti-God of painting" (GW, 46). Recalling the importance of the aesthetics of painting for the novelist Doderer—"reality is found on the surface"—the negative aura surrounding Ephraim Halfon seems quite important, and the revelations of the old painter contribute to Dr. Halfon's troubled relationship with his "father," whom he blames for the death of his mother.

The next chapter follows Halfon's fate, describing his induction into the military service, his work as a physician at the Russian front, his uneventful capture by an exceedingly polite and understanding Russian physician-officer, his assimilation into Russian life, and his relative happiness in his solitary existence. By the end of this chapter we have followed the first protagonist into the vastness of the Siberian landscape.

The next four chapters trace the life of Heinrich Zienhammer from his birth in 1865 in the village of Gross-Schweyntzkreuth to a Siberian prisoner-of-war camp in 1919, where Zienhammer betrays the nine Hungarian officers. The name of Zienhammer's imaginary home town includes rather unappetizing allusions to pigs—and possibly toads—and even Zienhammer is at one time called *unser Schwein* by the narrator.

Zienhammer is characterized as a man who has a quick mind and is a firstrate sharpshooter, but whose depth of understanding or perception is limited. He can talk himself out of embarrassing situations by skillful omissions and slight adjustments without actually lying. His glibness astounds Zienhammer himself. He is variously called a "hermit," a "cold swamp," or someone who "functions well" (GW, 73 - 74). In a diary entry on January 4, 1966, Doderer noted: "Zienhammer is a true representative of our time: a man of routine, impotent indifference [*impotente Wurstigkeit*], who can't be addressed [*unansprechbar*] or attacked: it is therefore quite normal that he wins, that he annihilates what gets in his way" (GW, 263).

An important aspect of Zienhammer's character is his inaccessibility and what Doderer might have called his lack of Eros.

Zienhammer is bothered and even frightened by open spaces, and at one point the expanse of the Prater meadows almost produces an attack of agoraphobia in him. He is equally uncomfortable in the vastness of Siberia. And during his first sexual adventure—on a visit to Vienna in 1882—the windows are closed and the muslin curtains drawn (GW, 71). This latter fact is emphasized by Doderer again and again, and the sense of being closed in or shut off becomes part of the signature of Zienhammer's character.

Much of chapters five and six is taken up with descriptions of Zienhammer's and other prisoners' lives and their abortive transport (or "shipment" as Doderer likes to call it) to the West. The details of camp life—based on Doderer's own experiences—emerge with authentic detail. Cafés, clubs, study groups, chamber music evenings, and first rate orchestras gave the life of the Austro-Hungarian prisoners surprisingly cultured and unprisonlike aspects. However, the brutality of the civil war and the succession of struggles between "white" and "red" forces constitutes a background that emphasizes both the adventure and the cheapness of human life.

Historical events intrude only occasionally into the narrative, unlike in the earlier novel, *Das Geheimnis des Reiches*, where long passages were devoted to historiography. Instead Doderer describes the remarkable financial success of the "operator" Zienhammer, who manages a lumber business with considerable profit. During this phase of his life, Zienhammer is described as a serious man who "doesn't read novels" (GW, 135), and who happens also be a reincarnation of another of Doderer's heroes: Julius Zihal, the well-functioning, dehumanized civil servant, beholden only to an impersonal set of legal guidelines.

Zienhammer's betrayal of nine fellow officers, with whom he had studied Hungarian once a week in order to improve himself, should be seen within the context of the depersonalized behavior of the perpetrator. In his *Abwesenheit* (absence [of mind]) Zienhammer frequently acts like an automaton, unaware of good or evil. He simply functions when called upon. When the leader of the vengeful and brutal "Czech Legion" demands that he should identify the names of nine Hungarian officers who are spuriously accused of subversive activities, Zienhammer performs without thinking.

However, he reveals a residual sense of guilt, in that he fears someone will witness the betrayal. His fearful glances focus on a pale face which stares at him from a window nearby. Zienhammer does not know that it is the face of Ernst von Rottenstein, who is to become his antagonist. The description of the face focuses on the eyes: "The glance from dark eyes was directed exactly at him. This glance was entirely still, unmoved, competely quiet: taking in what he saw without contradiction, and keeping it. Everything" (GW, 170).

Seen from Zienhammer's point of view, the face evokes guilt. Zienhammer does not know that the witness interprets what he sees in a way quite different from what actually happened. Doderer's emphasis on relativizing events through using different perspectives and through withholding authorial omniscience was intended to be part of the technique of his *roman muet*.

In the seventh chapter, an interlude on the theme of memory and forgetting indicates both the despicable nature of Zienhammer's act and, as an alternative to his behavior, the fate of the martyr. In an author's aside, Doderer tells of Elsa Brandström, a Swedish Red Cross Nurse who was known as the Angel of Siberia, and who fought bravely for the lives of the nine Hungarian officers. Doderer's message is clear: faced with the alternative of betrayal or death, the choice should be death.

Repeating almost word for word the passage from the end of the first chapter, Doderer notes that, given the continuity of consciousness, there is no undisturbed forgetting. The symbolic expression of the past is the image of the "water of time [which] stands clear, layer upon layer, decade upon decade" (GW, 174).

To describe the scene of the meeting between Zienhammer and Thamar Halfon, Doderer includes a rapid flashback to Vienna in 1882, this time from the perspective of the woman. Living unhappily with a much older and terrifyingly severe husband, Thamar Halfon seduces the young Heinrich Zienhammer, picking him quite literally off the street: "She had robbed what she needed and she carried it with her: and thus also the possibility to continue living with Ephraim Halfon" (GW, 175). After what she feels to be the fulfilling of her function—giving birth to Alfons Halfon—she gradually loses the desire to live and drifts into death. Again, the motif of the border forest is associated with her death: "There also was a young forest, actually more a little forest [*Wäldchen*]. She entered it. It received her. Oh yes! That is what mattered for her; and not whether one went to the theater or one would receive guests" (GW, 176).

Chapters eight and nine introduce Ernst von Rottenstein, one of the intended central characters and witness to Zienhammer's crime. From the beginning Doderer stresses Rottenstein's eyes, his quiet stare, and his accurate memory. An accomplished pianist, Rottenstein can play long sonatas from memory even after an interval of years.

The motif of the forest is also associated with him. He can see small woods near the villa of his parents. This time Doderer emphasizes the realm beyond the forest: "Beyond the copse one suspected a lighter glow; it was impossible to recognize where the light came from, only the sky glanced brighter between the crowns of the trees" (GW, 178). This small stand of trees is also associated with the center of Rottenstein's existence during the years between graduation from the *Gymnasium* and the beginning of the war: the "boudoir" of his mother, which she hardly uses and which is pervaded by light. Doderer's penchant for symbolism of openness emphasizes the windows of this small room and the view from those windows. The scents surrounding his mother are also associated with the room, where the young man likes to sit for hours and stare from the window.

Rottenstein seems to have been intended as one of the ordinary-extraordinary protagonists which grace several of Doderer's novels. He looks like a "pretty Bohemian chamber maid," and in school he happens to be sitting next to a certain Doderer. Rottenstein is slightly languid and indifferent during his adolescence. Only when he reaches the university does he start to sense the beginning of something new. In sharp contrast to Zienhammer, Rottenstein grasps the largeness or spaciousness of existence, and he is not frightened by it (GW, 197). This grasp is by no means an intellectual understanding, but simply a sensitivity, or a positive emotional response, inchoate, but indicative of the general tendencies of Rottenstein's character. Rottenstein possesses one of the qualities of all of Doderer's positive protagonists: he is accessible (*zugänglich*).

Doderer carefully prepares the witness function of Rottenstein, and by retracing Rottenstein's life from his school years through his involvement in cavalry battles of the war to his life in Siberia, we gain yet another perspective on a fate similar to that of Ventruba, Alfons Halfon, and Zienhammer. The lines of action of Rottenstein's fate converge with those of Zienhammer's during the betrayal of the Hungarian officers. This time we see the event from the inside of the barracks, without any intimation of its despicable nature.

The fragment closes with the condemnation of Zienhammer by a Russian farmer, Yegorov, who has employed the traitor. With ceremonious words Yegorov indicts Zienhammer, calling him a "scabrous devil," adding that Zienhammer is "one of the hell's dogs

The Late Phase: facta loquuntur

allowed by this war to come up from the depths" (GW, 217). Yegorov has his sons and his dogs chase Zienhammer from his farm, and one of his sons hurls a stick at Zienhammer's back, which renders him unconscious. Dr. Halfon, whom fate has placed near the camp, comes by to find the unconscious man (who is his father), takes him to his home and quickly cures him. After Zienhammer's recuperation the fragment ends with Zienhammer's preparations for his return to the West.

Even though *Der Grenzwald* remained a fragment, its unity of tone and atmosphere emerges clearly. As Weber has pointed out in the *Nachwort* (GW, 271 - 72), the atmospheric qualities seemed to have been more important to Doderer than the surface plot. Clarification of the sometimes mysterious connections between the characters may not even have been intended. *Deperzeptive Existenz*, for which Zienhammer seems to be a prototype, constitutes one of the most fundamental themes of the torso. The narrative technique that serves this theme of limited sight and insight most aptly is that which Doderer has tagged *facta loquuntur*, the attempt to make unreflected facts speak for themselves and to reduce the interpolations or the presence of a narrator-commentator to a minimum. In that sense *Der Grenzwald* represents the closest approximation to the *roman muet*.

CHAPTER 7

Conclusion

DODERER has created a unique and substantial *oeuvre*. His writing is imbued with local color, with historical breadth and mystical depth. Scornful of utopian thinking and allergic to any hint of ideology, he spurned literary trends that went in the direction of unmitigated doom or of expansive formlessness.

A thoroughly learned historian, he knew in detail the rich traditions of literature, of the arts, and of philosophy. Homer, the Patristic writers, scholasticism, medieval historiography, Latin humanism, as well as the prose of the nineteenth century live in his work in visible ways.

His language is enriched by the style of an earlier eccentric, Jean Paul, with whom he shares a penchant for irony. The tragic farce of Johann Nestroy reverberates in Doderer's novels, and yet he knows the resignation and detachment of Adalbert Stifter. In virtuosity of language, in delicate and occasionally bawdy humor, and in aristocratic haughtiness combined with homespun cordiality he has no equal among novelists writing in German.

To the conventional ideal of *Bildung*, and thus to the *Bildungsroman*, Doderer gave a personal twist. The social, intellectual, and moral shaping of a young person becomes in his writing more down-to-earth and—this is the twist—more accidental. *Bildung* becomes *Menschwerdung*. Learning may be a necessary part of this process—Leonhard Kakabsa studies Latin—but it is not sufficient by itself. Emotional commitment may be a part as well—Melzer learns to love Thea Rokitzer—but neither does that seem to suffice. Nor is *Menschwerdung* in Doderer's novels and stories necessarily followed by suggestions of successful integration into society. It is rather an intensely personal event, often associated with a sudden, nonrational—perhaps mystical—insight. It may—as in *Des letzte Abenteuer*—be followed by the hero's death, or as in *Die Strudlhofstiege*, by a happy end. Regardless of how the conver-

Conclusion

sion takes place, it is Doderer's tentative admission of the possibility of change; tentative because most of his characters seem to be victims of unchanging and predetermined fate.

Through the image of railroad tracks Doderer has expressed the inflexible nature of fate, and although few of his characters are ever derailed or—in this specific sense—switched, Doderer's determinism does not turn into gloom. Beginning and end may be fixed; nevertheless, life acquires richness and perhaps decorum in the twists, turns, and detours that divert from the direct path between birth and death.

With this in mind we must see the central symbol of *Die Strudlhofstiege*. The steps signify the importance of the transformation of what was once an unadorned hillside into a work of civilization. Descending the steps, in contrast to sliding down the hill, is a gesture of dignified and civilized behavior.

In his admission of the possibility of change and choice Doderer is distinct from many major novelists of the twentieth century. One need only invoke the name of Franz Kafka in order to exemplify the trend of depicting images in inexorable fate that are embedded in a barely knowable world. Doderer is by no means blind to social ills or private and collective evils; rather he attempts to transcend mere description or diagnosis of evil. A character such as Schlaggenberg in *Die Dämonen* may be caught up in his private demonology, which may in turn stand for collective blindness, but in the end he is shaken sufficiently to revert to clearer apperception of himself and his problems.

The uncluttering of perception is probably the most frequent theme of Doderer's novels. In many metaphoric disguises, Doderer attempts to demonstrate the importance of *Apperception*, which in his moral universe is equated with virtue, whereas its opposite, *Apperceptions-Verweigerung*, is sin. The novels serve a moralistic purpose in that Doderer wants the reader to learn to see clearly. In that sense, his writing serves an extraliterary purpose. As he indicated in an interview with Palma Caetano: "I became a writer because I felt that that was the way to come to grips with life. . ." (. . .*mit dem Leben fertig werden*. . .).

Throughout his novels, Doderer symbolizes spiritual health through metaphors of access, especially windows and eyes. The opposite is frequently suggested by closed rooms, drawn curtains, or impenetrable walls. The condition of being accessible is sometimes manifested in surprisingly banal ways, as in Leonhard Kakabsa's sudden feeling that he was born to smell. With instinctual certainty he senses, from that time on, that there is something different about him, and his Old World bootstrap program of self-taught Latin is only Doderer's quixotic way of symbolizing a fundamental change. Kakabsa's behavior is guided effortlessly by his sense of identity, a phenomenon which Doderer has tagged with either the scholastic principle of *operari sequitur esse* or the formula of *lebensgemäss denken*. Thinking in harmony with knowable reality and refraining from attempts to shape reality according to preconceived ideas become guiding principles of Doderer's morality.

The high seriousness with which Doderer endowed his work must be appreciated when approaching his writing. Doderer felt that therapy through literature could only be achieved by realistic or naturalistic novels. In the epilogue to the Reclam edition of *Das letzte Abenteuer* he asserts apodictically: ". . .One thing can only be achieved by the naturalistic novel, which uses the ingredients offered by everyday life: to render weightless all the terror or jumble [*Schrecken oder Klimbim*], to suspend it, and finally to transform the forever identical walls which enclose us, into windows through which we look outside, while transcendence—evident because of the quite trivial frame—shines in."

Perhaps we may find this claim to be grandiose. Yet, juxtaposed with the pomposity of theories which exaggerate the self-sufficiency of art, Doderer's ideas hark back to the more modest Classical demand of *prodesse et delectare*. In spite, or perhaps because, of his dedication to writing, Doderer saw and sensed the difference between life and art, between the fictional and the created world, of which Someone Else at one time said repeatedly that it was good.

Notes and References

Preface

1. Peter Demetz, *Postwar German Literature* (New York, 1970), p. 229.
2. Ivar Ivask, "Heimito von Doderer's *Die Dämonen*," *Books Abroad* 31 (1957): 365.
3. George Steiner, "The Brown Danube," *Reporter*, October 12, 1961, p. 60.
4. Heinz Politzer, "Heimito von Doderer's *Demons* and the Modern Kakanian Novel," in *The Contemporary Novel in German*, ed. Robert H. Heitner (Austin and London, 1967), p. 61.
5. Ivask, loc. cit.

Chapter One

1. Karl Hopf, "Heimito von Doderer's Geburtsstätte," *Literatur und Kritik* 80 (December 1973): 621.
2. Horst Wiemer, "Damals im Verlag mit Heimito," in *Erinnerungen an Heimito von Doderer*, ed. Xaver Schaffgotsch (Munich, 1972), p. 186 (henceforth cited as Erinn, with page number in text).
3. Heimito von Doderer, "My Nineteen *Curricula Vitae*," *Chicago Review* 26: 2 (1974): trans. Vincent Kling, 84 - 85. (references to translations in this journal will henceforth be given as ChiR, with page number in the text).
4. Ernst Alker, "Die Jahre mit Doderer," Erinn, 16.
5. Heimito von Doderer, *The Demons*, trans. Richard and Clara Winston (New York, 1961), p. 1302 (future references will be abbreviated ThD, and the page number given in the text). Although this thought is ascribed to René von Stangeler, Doderer's alter ego in the novel, we can safely identify it with the author's feelings.
6. Journal 1. Heft, from Fall 1920, Ser. n. ("Series nova") 14.061. Typed and collated copies of Doderer's Journals, diaries, Commentarii, Nachtbücher, as well as typed copies of some letters were made available to me through the gracious cooperation of Frau Maria von Doderer and the invaluable assistance of Professor Wendelin Schmidt-Dengler, who has established a Doderer Archive at the Institut für Germanistik of the University of Vienna.
7. *Tangenten* (Munich, 1964), p. 617 (henceforth cited as T, with page number in text).

8. *Roman No 7: Zweiter Teil: Der Grenzwald* (Munich, 1967), p. 244 (henceforth cited as GW, with page number in text).
9. In a letter to the Germanist Dietrich Weber, August 28, 1960, Doderer Archive.
10. ". . .Von dem grossen russischen Bauernvolk, dessen Herz weit und offen ist, wie die Steppe. . . ," copy in the Doderer Archive.
11. The influence of Arthur Schopenhauer is discussed in an *Exkurs* in Dietrich Weber, *Heimito von Doderer: Studien zu seinem Romanwerk* (Munich, 1963), pp. 267 - 69 (henceforth cited as DW, with page number in text).
12. Heimito Doderer (sic), *Gassen und Landschaft* ([Vienna]: Haybach Verlag, [1923]), n. pag. Poems are numbered. Poem 24: "Aus Dir stürmen die Züge hinaus. / Aus Deinem Mund von Glas und Stahl entlässt Du nach vorwärts/den, dessen Leben einmal/ein Stück auf Reise und Strecke fiel." Reprinted in *Ein Weg im Dunklen* (Munich, 1957), p. 22.
13. Poem 2: "Hier kommt die Schönste aller Schönen—es freut mich herzlich, dass Du pünktlich bist:/sonst an die Mätzchen will ich mich gewöhnen."
14. As an example for the tone of Doderer's diaries this entry deserves to be quoted in the original: "Was ist das Schönste, der herrlichste Zustand? Das Schönste ist, wenn Dein Hirn sich rasend bemüht, das Material, welches von unten heraufgetrieben wird (noch so roh, in Blöcken, barbarisch-primitiven Bildern) zu spalten, zu durchdringen endlich — es auszudrücken. Gegen diesen Zustand gehalten, sind alle Freuden und Wollüste, die sich nur erdenken lassen, schäbiger Katzendreck."
15. "Tagebuch eines Schriftstellers," 1925 - 26, Ser. n. 14.066. Doderer Archive.
16. *Frühe Prosa*, ed. Hans Flesch-Brunningen (Munich, 1968), p. 7 (henceforth cited as FP, with page number in text).
17. Journal 2. Heft, Ser. 1. 14.062. On November 16, 1922, he writes: "Von [Freud] beziehe ich jetzt meine Weisheiten." Doderer Archive.
18. *Die Dämonen* begins—after the *Ouvertüre*—with a chapter entitled "Draussen am Rande," translated in the English edition as "On the Outskirts of the City." The idea of approaching events from the periphery, which is as telling as the center, is later developed into a principle of Doderer's compositions.
19. "Erst bricht man Fenster. Dann wird man selbst eines." *Meine neunzehn Lebensläufe und neun andere Geschichten* (Munich, 1966), p. 10. Cf. also *ChiR*, 79 - 85.
20. *Commentarii 1951 bis 1956*, ed. Wendelin Schmidt-Dengler (Munich, 1976), p. 451 (henceforth cited as C, with page number in text).
21. Cf. "Grundlagen und Funktion des Romans" in *Die Wiederkehr der Drachen*, ed. Wendelin Schmidt-Dengler (Munich, 1970), esp. p. 167 (this collection of essays is henceforth referred to as WdD, with page numbers in the text).
22. "Die Aufgabe, die sich dem Roman heute stellt, ist. . .die Wiedereroberung der Aussenwelt: und in dieser wird bekanntlich

Notes and References

gehandelt, in jedem Sinne. . . . Der utopische oder transreale Roman, wie ihn die Deutschen immer wieder hervorbringen, kann jene angegebene Funktion nicht erfüllen." WdD, 169.

23. Cf. a letter written by Doderer's last secretary, Wolfgang H. Fleischer, cited in FP, 371 - 72, and especially Wendelin Schmidt-Dengler, "Heimito von Doderers 'Jutta Bamberger' Entstehung, Aufbau, Thematik," *Zeitschrift für deutsche Philologie* 89: 4 (1970): 576 - 601.

24. Ibid., p. 576.

25. Ibid., p. 581.

26. "Tagebuch eines Schriftstellers," February 1926, cites from the second of Rilke's "Sonnets to Orpheus: "Wo ist ihr Tod? O, wirst du dies Motiv/erfinden noch, eh sich dein Lied verzehrte?—/Wo sinkt sie hin aus mir? . . .Ein Mädchen fast. . . ."

27. Journal 3. Heft, Ser. n. 14.063, entry from July 28, 1923.

28. Entries speculating on the artistic techniques of cinematography are found in Doderer's journals from 1922 on. *In Tagebuch eines Schriftstellers*, Ser. n. 14.066 (1925 - 26), Doderer attempts to identify film techniques that could be used for prose narrative, and he specifies, among others: "1.) Ausdruck durch die sprechenden Tatsachen—nicht meditativ! 2.) Kühnheit des sprunghaften Bildwechsels. 3.) Knappe, zusammengeraffte Kompositionsart." The influence of film on Doderer's compositional technique has not yet been explored.

29. Michael Hamburger, *From Prophecy to Exorcism* (London, 1965), p. 139.

30. Doderer's theory of apperception, as well as his ideas concerning ideologies, or antiideologies, in fact his conservative, quasi-aristocratic stance have come under increasing attack, especially by Hans Joachim Schröder, Anton Reininger, and to some extent by Frank Trommler. See annotated bibliography.

31. Journal, 3. Heft, Ser. n. 14.063.

32. "Heute glaube ich, dass theoretische Auseinanderlegung nichts nützt in Fragen der "Erzählung": immerhin kann man die Richtlinien getrost bewusst machen! Wesentlich aber: intensive Anschauung während der Gestaltung. Gesetz wächst von selbst aus der Praxis."

33. Journal, 3. Heft, November 1923. "Was mich am meisten ärgert ist Knechtschaft, die dem Novellisten Gegenständliches auferlegt, Fabel, kurz: die Geschichte, welche man erzählt."

34. Journal, 3. Heft. "Lauschen, nicht lärmen! Die Wirklichkeit (Gott) ist so still: wir verzerren sie in unserem Vorder-Grund-Leben."

35. Journal, 3. Heft, 1923. "Es handelt sich darum, dass man stets dem Strom des Lebens nahebleibe, dass man sich nicht in Seitenkanäle verliere, in "Urteilen" stagniere, in "Ansichten" festlege, im Äusserlichen decidiere und beschränke: vielmehr ist gegenüber alledem notorische Gleichgültigkeit das einzig Wahre!"

36. *Die Erzählungen*, ed. Wendelin Schmidt-Dengler (Munich, 1972), p. 55. Henceforth cited as E, with page number in text.

37. "Tagebuch eines Schriftstellers," Ser. n. 14.066 (1925 - 26).

38. WdD, 158: "Es brauchte sich einer nur wirklich zu erinnern und er wäre ein Dichter."

Chapter Two

1. A list of Doderer's miscellaneous theoretical and critical writings has been compiled by Wendelin Schmidt-Dengler and published in the *Anhang* to WdD, 313 - 22.
2. Paris von Gütersloh, *Bekenntnisse eines modernen Malers* (Vienna, Leipzig, 1926). Original title *Meine grosse und kleine Geschichte: Eine Lebensbeschreibung quasi un'allegoria*. Cf. also WdD, 95 (henceforth cited as Bek., with page number in text).
3. Cf. Ivar Ivask, "Heimito von Doderer: An Introduction," *Wisconsin Studies in Contemporary Literature* 7 (Autumn 1967): 529. See also WdD, 135 - 36.
4. E. G.: ". . .Als ob es sich darum handelte, uns eine Tracht Wissen auf den für den Hintern geltenden Kopf zu versetzen. . . ."
5. Cf. WdD, 122: "Sein Wesen. . . , dass er garnicht mehr den Versuch macht, das Sinnlose durch Sinngebung à tout prix zu integrieren."
6. WdD, 123: "Es gibt im totalen Roman keine Haupt- und Begleitstimmen, viel weniger noch wie in der Kontrapunktik, die doch irgendwo hinauswill."
7. WdD, 123: "Der totale Roman sollte die Welt sehen mit einem fast schon verglasten Auge, welches alsbald nach oben brechen und in das sich dann nur mehr der leere Himmel schlagen wird. Jedoch dieser Augenblick des Abschieds, wo man noch ganz da ist, aber durchaus nichts mehr will, müsste wohl auch einzigartig sehend machen."
8. WdD, 64: ". . .Das Tun (und somit auch das Werk) kommt aus dem Sein."
9. Dietrich Weber calls it "polygraphisch," and Ivar Ivask calls it "panoramic."
10. José Antonio Palma Caetano, "The Short Stories of Heimito von Doderer," *BA* 42 (1968): 363 - 65. C. discusses "Leon Pujot," "Ein sicherer Instinkt," and "Der Brand."
11. Vincent Kling, trans., ChiR, 97 - 106. This translation contains some minor mistakes.
12. A graphic representation of "Zwei Lügen" is given in Journal, from March 4, 1932, Ser. n. 14.069.
13. "'Le Malentendu' und Doderer's 'Zwei Lügen,'" *Archiv* 208 (1971): 23 - 24.
14. Knust, p. 29.
15. Palma Caetano, "Short Stories," p. 365.
16. Cf. *Autobiographisches Nachwort* to the Reclam edition of *Das letzte Abenteuer*, esp. p. 126.
17. "Water Imagery in Doderer's Novels," *BA* 42 (1968): 348 - 53.

18. *Das letzte Abenteuer* (Stuttgart, 1964), p. 26 (henceforth cited as D1A, with page number in text).
19. Sylvia Hayward-Jones, "Fate, Guilt and Freedom in Heimito von Doderer's *Ein Mord den jeder begeht* and *Ein Umweg*," *German Life and Letters* 14 (April 1961): 163.
20. Heimito von Doderer, *Ein Umweg* (Munich, 1940), p. 42 (henceforth cited as U, with page number in text).

Chapter Three

1. Commentarii Aug./Sept. 1937, Ser. n. 14.074, in the Doderer Archive in Vienna.
2. *Ein Mord den jeder begeht* (Munich, 1938), p. 5 (henceforth abbreviated as "Mord"). The English translation, *Every Man a Murderer*, trans. Richard and Clara Winston (New York, 1964), is cited as "M" with page numbers in the text.
3. In the following I am loosely following my article in *Modern Language Studies*, "Chaos, Order and Humanization in Doderer's Early Works," V: 2 (Fall 1975): 68 - 77.
4. Munich, 1950, p. 8.
5. "Er spürte sozusagen das Stecken im oben zugebundenen Säckchen, das Stehen neben dem Leben." The image of the *Hautsack* is borrowed from Franz Blei, cf. WdD, 112.
6. "Kakanian" refers to the customary abbreviation "k.u.k.," which stood for "imperial and royal." It has come to signify the hierarchies and the bureaucratic life and world of the Austro-Hungarian Empire before World War I.

Chapter Four

1. WdD, 160: ". . .Einer, der weder an der Welt, noch an sich arbeiten will, wahrlich ein Mensch ohne Zielsetzungen."
2. Cf. esp. "The Theory of Romantic Poetry," in Hans Eichner, *Friedrich Schlegel* (New York, 1970), pp. 44 - 83.
3. *Repertorium*, ed. Dietrich Weber (Munich, 1969), p. 72 (henceforth cited as Rep, with page number in text).
4. "Heimito von Doderer," in *Deutsche Dichter der Gegenwart*, ed. Benno von Wiese (Berlin, 1972), pp. 46 - 63.
5. Roswitha Fischer has described the genesis of this novel with painstaking accuracy in *Studien zur Entstehungsgeschichte der "Strudlhofstiege" Heimito von Doderers*, Wiener Arbeiten zur Deutschen Literatur (Vienna, 1975).
6. "For a Literary Epic the Place is Vienna, the Time the Late Twenties," pp. 4 - 5, 38.
7. Morton, p. 4.

8. Ibid., p. 38.
9. Ibid.
10. Ibid.
11. "Books of the Times," September 25, 1961.
12. "Translations: Sad Splendor," p. 91.
13. "The Brown Danube," October 12, 1961, pp. 58, 60.
14. Steiner, p. 60.
15. Ibid.
16. Ibid.
17. "Huge, Fine Novel of a City That Was," p. 4.
18. *BA* 31 (1957): 365.
19. For challenging criticism of Doderer's handling of the narrator(s) cf. Martin W. Swales, "The Narrator in the Novels of Heimito von Doderer," *Modern Language Review* LXI (1966): 85 - 95.
20. On the topic of language as theme cf. Wendelin Schmidt-Dengler, "Die Thematisierung der Sprache in Heimito von Doderers *Die Dämonen*," in *Sprachthematik in der österreichischen Literatur des 20. Jahrhunderts* (Vienna, 1974), pp. 119 - 34.
21. From "Nachtbuch," Ser. n. 14.102, from August 21, 1954: ". . .Ich lieg wie begraben und bin überall wie Erde unter dieser wimmelnden Masse der Stadt, die ich gleich einer Decke über mich gezogen hatte: das ist die Entstehung und Funktion der 'Dämonen.' " Doderer Archive, Vienna.

Chapter Five

1. For the chronology of the shorter prose works, see the editor's *Anhang* in E, 497 - 501.
2. "Heimito von Doderers 'Posaunen von Jericho,' " *Philologische Studien und Quellen* 60 (Berlin, 1971).
3. "Realismus und Realität in Heimito von Doderers *Posaunen von Jericho*," *Germanic Review* 38: 1 (January 1963): 40.
4. Politzer, p. 46.
5. Ibid., p. 49.
6. Ibid.
7. "Doderer's *Posaunen von Jericho*," *Symposium* 21 (Summer 1967): 151.
8. Tschirky, pp. 67 - 68.
9. C, 35: "In den 'Merowingern' werde ich mir eine Reservation für das Groteske schaffen, das mir sonst überal Unfug treibt. . . ."
10. Unpublished, in the Doderer Archive, Vienna.
11. Letter to Dietrich Weber.
12. Swales, loc. cit., 88.
13. In *Dichter der Gegenwart*, p. 53.
14. Cf. esp. C, 185.
15. *Die Merowinger oder Die totale Familie* (Munich, 1962), pp. 230 - 31 (henceforth cited as MER, with page number in text).

Notes and References

Chapter Six

1. Lutz-Werner Wolff, *Wiedereroberte Aussenwelt*, Göppinger Arbeiten zur Germanistik, Nr. 13 (Göppingen, 1969), p. 47.
2. *Deutsche Literatur seit 1945* (Stuttgart, 1968), p. 84.
3. *Die Wasserfälle von Slunj* (Munich, 1963), pp. 134 - 35 (henceforth abbreviated WvS, with page number in text). The English translation, *The Waterfalls of Slunj*, trans. Eithne Wilkins and Ernst Kaiser (New York, 1966), is cited as WoS, with page number in text.
4. "Water Imagery in Doderer's Novels," *BA* 42 (Summer 1968): 349 ff.
5. For an interesting discussion of the *Krebs* motif cf. Lutz-Werner Wolff, pp. 204 - 12.
6. Haberl, *BA* 42, p. 349.
7. Cited by Lutz-Werner Wolff, p. 113: "Der Blick vom apperzeptiven Leser auf die deperzeptive Existenz: das ist R[oman] [No.] 7."
8. Cf. esp. Lutz-Werner Wolff, p. 106 ff.
9. (Munich, 1967), with an epilogue by Dietrich Weber (henceforth cited as GW, with page number in text).
10. Ivask, *Wisconsin Studies* 8 (1967): 535.
11. Lurz-Werner Wolff, p. 225.

Selected Bibliography

PRIMARY SOURCES

1. Unpublished *Tagebücher, Journale, Commentarii,* a *Nachtbuch, Skizzen,* and some private correspondence are collected, typed, and collated in the Doderer Archive, under the care of Dr. Wendelin Schmidt-Dengler of the Germanistisches Institut of the University of Vienna.

2. Doderer's essays on literary, philosophical, and historical topics, his reviews, and some of his speeches are enumerated in the *Anhang* to *Wiederkehr der Drachen.* They number 207, and copies of most of them are in the Doderer Archive.

3. A bibliography of Doderer's own major readings is found in Hans Joachim Schröder, *Apperzeption und Vorurteil.* Untersuchungen *zur Reflexion Heimito von Doderers* (Heidelberg, 1976), pp. 454 - 56.

4. Major Works Published between 1923 and 1967
Das letzte Abenteuer. Mit einem autobiographischen Nachwort. Stuttgart: Reclam, 1964.
Die Dämonen. Nach der Chronik des Sektionsrates Geyrenhoff. Munich: Biederstein, 1956.
Die erleuchteten Fenster oder die Menschwerdung des Amtsrates Julius Zihal. Munich: Biederstein, 1950.
Die Merowinger oder Die totale Familie. Munich: Biederstein, 1962.
Die Strudlhofstiege oder Melzer und die Tiefe der Jahre. Munich: Biederstein, 1951.
Ein Mord den jeder begeht. Munich: Biederstein, 1938.
Ein Umweg. Munich: Biederstein, 1940.
Ein Weg im Dunklen: Gedichte und epigrammatische Verse. Munich: Biederstein, 1957.
Gassen und Landschaft. [Vienna]: Haybach Verlag, [1923].
Meine neunzehn Lebensläufe und neun andere Geschichten. (Mit neunzehn Photographien und einer Schallplatte.) Munich: Biederstein, 1966.
Roman No 7, Erster Teil: Die Wasserfälle von Slunj. Munich: Biederstein, 1963.
Roman No 7, Zweiter Teil: Der Grenzwald (Fragment). (Nachwort von Dietrich Weber.) Munich: Biederstein, 1967.

Selected Bibliography

Tangenten: Tagebuch eines Schriftstellers 1940 - 1950. Munich: Biederstein, 1964.

5. Editions Published after Doderer's Death

FLESCH-BRUNNINGEN, HANS, ed. *Frühe Prosa: Die Bresche/Jutta Bamberger/Das Geheimnis des Reiches*. Munich: Biederstein, 1968.

KRAMBERG, KARL HEINZ, ed. *Das Doderer-Buch: Eine Auswahl aus seinem Werk*. Munich: Biederstein, 1976.

SCHMIDT-DENGLER, WENDELIN, ed. *Commentarii 1951 bis 1956: Tagebücher aus dem Nachlass*. Munich: Biederstein, 1976.

———. *Die Erzählungen*. Munich: Biederstein, 1972.

———. *Die Wiederkehr der Drachen: Aufsätze/Traktate/Reden*. Introd. Wolfgang H. Fleischer. Munich: Biederstein, 1970.

WEBER, DIETRICH, ed. *Repertorium: Ein Begreifbuch von höheren und niederen Lebens-Sachen*. Munich: Biederstein, 1969.

6. English Translations

IVASK, ASTRID, trans. "The Magician's Art." *Literary Review* 5 (1961): 5 - 17.

———. "Two Short Stories: Stepfield and Sonatina." *Literary Review* 6 (1962 - 63): 176 - 80.

KLING, VINCENT, trans. "The Trumpets of Jericho," "Under Black Stars," "A Person Made of Porcelain," "My Nineteen *Curricula Vitae*," "Two Lies or Classical Tragedy in a Village," "from: The Strudlhof Steps," *Chicago Review* 26 (1974): 5 - 138.

ROSEN, ROBERT S., trans. "The Torment of the Leather Pouches." *Odyssey Review* 3 (March 1963): 219 - 32.

WILKINS, EITHNE, and KAISER, ERNST, trans. *The Waterfalls of Slunj*. New York: Harcourt, Brace, 1966.

WINSTON, RICHARD and CLARA, trans. *The Demons* (2 vols.). New York: Knopf, 1961.

———. *Every Man a Murderer*. New York: Knopf, 1964.

SECONDARY SOURCES

1. No comprehensive bibliography of Doderer criticism exists to date. Several partial listings are available:

"Bio-Bibliography of Heimito von Doderer." Compiled by Ivar Ivask. *Books Abroad* 42: 3 (Summer 1968): 380 - 84.

SCHMIDT-DENGLER, WENDELIN. "Bibliographie: Sekundärliteratur zu Heimito von Doderer." *Literatur und Kritik* 80 (December 1973): 615 - 20.

WEBER, DIETRICH. "Anhang II: Heimito von Doderer — Eine Bibliographie." In Dietrich Weber, *Heimito von Doderer. Studien zu seinem Romanwerk* (Munich, 1963), pp. 298 - 320.

2. The following listing makes no claim to completeness, and the absence of commentary is not to be construed in a negative way.

"The Austrian Scene." *(London) Times Literary Supplement*, August 16, 1957, p. x. Stresses that Doderer is not an intellectual writer like Thomas Mann or Hesse or Musil, but one who is preoccupied with motive and action, with ideology and moral responsibility.

BACHEM, MICHAEL. "Chaos, Order and Humanization in Doderer's Early Works." *Modern Language Studies* 5:2 (1975), 68 - 77.

BITHELL, JETHRO. *Modern German Literature 1880 - 1950* (London: Methuen ed. 2, 1959), pp. 504 - 13. General English introduction to Doderer, including *Die Dämonen*.

BLAUHUT, ROBERT. "Heimito von Doderer, der Dichter des Kairos. Analyse seiner Novellen." *Wort in der Zeit* 7/8 (1964): 69 - 77.

BOELCESKVY, ANDREW. "Spatial Form and Moral Ambiguity: A Note on Heimito von Doderer's Narrative Technique." *German Quarterly* 47 (1974): 55 - 59.

BUDDEBERG, ELSE. " 'Schreibe, als ob du allein im Universum wärest.' Zu Heimito von Doderer: *Tagebuch eins Schriftstellers 1940 - 50.*" *Deutsche Beiträge zur geistigen Überlieferung* 7 (1972): 160 - 239.

CRISTOPHE, JEAN-PIERE. "Heimito von Doderer ou la rehabilitation du roman." *Revue d' Allemagne* 3 (1971): 903 - 15.

DEMETZ, PETER. *Postwar German Literature. A Critical Introduction.* New York: Western Publishing Company, 1970, pp. 229 - 41.

"Der Spätzünder." *Der Spiegel*, June 5, 1957, pp. 53 - 58. Breezy but informative reaction to Doderer, after the publication of *Die Dämonen*.

DOPPLER, ALFRED. "Historische Ereignisse im österreichischen Roman." In his *Wirklichkeit im Spiegel der Sprache*. Vienna: Europa Verlag, 1975, pp. 172 - 96. Stresses Doderer's unswerving faith in the adequacy of language and its metaphors in rendering a reliable portrait of reality.

EISENREICH, HERBERT. "Heimito von Doderer." In *Deutsche Dichter der Gegenwart. Ihr Leben und Werk.* Ed. Benno von Wiese. Berlin: Schmidt, 1972, pp. 46 - 63. Argues that Doderer wrote some of the most successful novels of the twentieth century. Eisenreich sounds convincing although he sometimes uses the master's stylistic mannerisms.

FISCHER, ROSWITHA. *Studien zur Entstehungsgeschichte und zum Aufbau der "Strudlhofstiege" Heimito von Doderers.* Wiener Arbeiten zur deutschen Literatur, 5. Vienna: Braumüller, 1975. (Diss. Vienna 1971.) Painstakingly thorough account of the genesis of *Die Strudlhofstiege,* utilizing all stages of diary entries, typescript, to finished novel.

FLEISCHMANN, WOLFGANG B. "A New Look at Austrian Literature." *America,* September 17, 1960, pp. 644 - 47. According to Fleischmann, Doderer's work provides a link between two groups of Austrian writers, the first consisting of Schnitzler, Werfel, Zweig, Roth, and Lernet-Holenia and the second of Musil and Broch.

HAMBURGER, MICHAEL. *From Prophecy to Exorcism.* London: Longmans,

Selected Bibliography

1965, pp. 131 - 39. Excellent sympathetic criticism, the key sentence of which is: "Unlike Thomas Mann in *Dr. Faustus,* Doderer's *The Demons* is a work that does not demonize evil, but de-demonizes evil by making it understandable."

HATFIELD, HENRY. "Vitality and Tradition: Two Novels by Heimito von Doderer." In his *Crisis and Continuity in Modern German Fiction.* Ithaca & London: Cornell University Press, 1969, pp. 90 - 108. Sensitive discussion of *Die Strudlhofstiege* and *Die Wasserfälle von Slunj,* stressing Doderer's craftsmanship, his delicate, lyrical sensibility, and the keenness of his psychological and moral awareness.

HAYWARD-JONES, SYLVIA. "Fate, Guilt and Freedom in Heimito von Doderer's *Ein Mord* and *Ein Umweg.*" *German Life and Letters* 14 (April 1961): 160 - 64.

HOPF, KARL. "Von der *Strudlhofstiege* zum *Grenzwald:* Die Funktion der Topographie in den Romanen Heimito von Doderers." *Österreich in Geschichte und Literatur* 16 (1972): 436 - 57.

HORST, KARL AUGUST. "Die Dämonie der zweiten Wirklichkeit." *Merkur* 10 (1956): 1005 - 14. Investigation of Doderer's use of *Ereignispsychologie:* how does a person react to a brutal fact, as for example Mary K. to the loss of a leg? *Dämonie* is discussed as neither a good nor evil force, but an aspect of character. Intercession of a personal *daimon* becomes evident in the reaction to an external event. In that moment there is an opportunity to (re)act freely.

IVASK, IVAR. "Heimito von Doderer: An Introduction." *Wisconsin Studies in Contemporary Literature* 8 (Autumn 1967): 528 - 47. Rich in biographical details, including personal communications. Superb account of plots.

─────, ed. Proceedings of "An International Symposium in Memory of Heimito von Doderer (1896 - 1966)." *Books Abroad* 42: 3 (Summer 1968): 343 - 84. Contributions by Ivar Ivask, Franz P. Haberl ("Water Imagery in Doderer's Novels"), Henry Hatfield ("The Human Tragicomedy: Doderer's *Die Wasserfälle von Slunj*"), David L. Jones ("A Quest for Tolerance"), Hans Flesch-Brunningen ("Heimito"), José Antonio Palma Caetano ("The Short Stories of Heimito von Doderer"), Wendelin Schmidt-Dengler ("On the Posthumous Papers of Heimito von Doderer"), Martin Swales ("Doderer as Realist"), and H. M. Waidson ("Heimito von Doderer: 'Das letzte Abenteuer' ").

─────. "Psychologie und Geschichte in Doderers Romanwerk." *Literatur und Kritik* 24 (May 1968): 213 - 17. Facing basic, though perhaps unpleasant truths about human beings saves us from the shallowness of ideologies.

JONES, DAVID L. "Proust and Doderer as Historical Novelists." *Comparative Literature Studies* 10: 1 (1973): 9 - 23.

─────. "Proust and Doderer: Themes and Techniques." *Books Abroad* 37:1 (Winter 1963): 12 - 15. Concludes that Doderer is "anti-Proustian" in his treatment of memory. Proust is said to be most often the philosopher of time recaptured while Doderer remains the dramatist of time recaptured.

KLEIN, ULRICH. "Die Rolle übertragenen Sprechens (Vergleich, Metapher, Bild) bei Heimito von Doderer." *Wirkendes Wort* 19 (1969): 324 - 37.

KNUST, HERBERT. "Camus' *Le Malentendu* und Doderers *Zwei Lügen*." *Archiv für das Studium der Neueren Sprachen und Literaturen* 208 (1971): 23 - 34. Interesting juxtaposition of the treatment of the folkloristic motif of the returning son.

KRISPYN, EGBERT. "Die eigentliche Polizei: Zur Erzähl-Situation in Heimito von Doderers Roman *Die erleuchteten Fenster oder die Menschwerdung des Amtsrates Julius Zihal*." *Language and Style* 2:2 (1969): 132 - 42.

LARSEN, M. DEEN. "Heimito von Doderer: The Elusive Realist." *Chicago Review* 26:2 (1974): 55 - 69. Fine general introduction to Doderer in English.

LINDLEY, DENVER. "Huge, Final Novel of a City That Was." *Herald Tribune*, September 24, 1961. Reaction of an erudite general reader to *The Demons*.

MORTON, FREDERIC. "For a Literary Epic the Place Is Vienna, the Time the Late Twenties." *New York Times Book Review*, September 24, 1961, pp. 4 - 5, 38. Hails *The Demons* as a "genuine modern epic." Argues that Doderer's diagnosis of Western culture is more universally valid than that of Broch or Musil.

PABISCH, PETER KARL. "The Uniqueness of Austrian Literature: An Introductory Contemplation of Heimito von Doderer." *Chicago Review* 26:2 (1974): 86 - 96.

POLITZER, HEINZ. "Heimito von Doderer's *Demons* and the Modern Kakanian Novel." In *The Contemporary Novel in German*. Ed. Robert H. Heitner. Austin & London: University of Texas Press, 1967, pp. 37 - 62.

———. "Realismus und Realität in Heimito von Doderers *Posaunen von Jericho*." *Germanic Review* 38:1 (January 1963): 37 - 51. One of the best articles on Doderer. Politzer stresses the tentative, unbourgeois, cautious relationship of Doderer to truth, morality, and cognition. Politzer also sees absurd, surreal, and grotesque elements, which few other critics have pointed to.

———. "Zeit, Wirklichkeit, Musik im Werk Heimito von Doderers." In his *Das Schweigen der Sirenen. Studien zur deutschen und österreichischen Literatur*. Stuttgart: Metzler, 1968, pp. 70 - 78.

PRESCOTT, ORVILLE. "Book of the Times." *New York Times*, September 25, 1961. Reaction to the publication of *The Demons*.

"A Re-awakened Culture. Fortune and Fortitude of Four District Traditions." *(London) Times Literary Supplement*, September 23, 1960.

REININGER, ANTON. *Die Erlösung des Bürgers: Eine ideologiekritische Studie zum Werk Heimito von Doderers*. Bonner Arbeiten zur deutschen Literatur, 30. Bonn: Bouvier, 1975. Gentle criticism of Doderer's conservative, antipolitical ideas, of his description of a society without overt political tensions, and of his denunciation of political and social action.

SCHAFFGOTSCH, XAVER, ed. *Erinnerungen an Heimito von Doderer.* Munich: Biederstein, 1972. Friends remembering Doderer. From anecdotal contributions by classmates to essential information. The Palma Caetano interview is especially important. Other contributions by Gustav End, Ernst Alker, Gottfried Berger, Franz Blauensteiner, Herbert Eisenreich, Wolfgang H. Fleischer, Hans Flesch von Brunningen, Anton Fuchs, Hartmann Goertz, Rudolf Haybach, Astrid Ivask, Ivar Ivask, Friedrich Qualtinger, Walter Rilla, Roman Rocek, Xaver Schaffgotsch, Ernst von Scharmitzer, Edmund Schüller, Hilde Spiel, Ilse Strobl-Luckmann, Astri von Stummer, Friedrich Torberg, Peter von Tramin, Dietrich Weber, Horst Wiemer, and Dorothea Zeemann

SCHMIDT-DENGLER, WENDELIN. "Die Thematisierung der Sprache in Heimito von Doderers *Die Dämonen.*" In *Sprachthematik in der österreichischen Literatur des 20. Jahrhunderts.* Vienna: 1974, pp. 119 - 34. Investigation of Doderer's treatment of language as theme. Especially important for the figure of Kakabsa from *The Demons.*

———. "Heimito von Doderers 'Jutta Bamberger': Entstehung, Aufbau, Thematik." *Zeitschrift für deutsche Philologie* 89 (1970): 576 - 601. Impeccably thorough analysis of *Jutta Bamberger.*

———. "Zum Nachlass Heimoto von Doderers." *Literatur und Kritik* 4 (1969): 177 - 80.

SCHRÖDER, HANS JOACHIM. *Apperzeption und Vorurteil: Untersuchungen zur Reflexion Heimito von Doderers.* Beiträge zur neueren Literaturgeschichte, 28. Heidelberg: Winter 1976. Challenging much of the laudatory Doderer criticism, Schröder examines Doderer's idea of apperception. He concludes that Doderer's novels demonstrate the ideology of self-deception and thus contribute nothing to either knowledge or criticism of reality. Includes an especially good bibliography of Doderer's own readings.

SHAW, MICHAEL. "Doderer's *Posaunen von Jericho.*" *Symposium* 21:2 (Summer 1967): 141 - 54. Disagreeing with Heinz Politzer, Shaw interprets *Posaunen* as a story of spiritual failure and subsequent healing.

———. "An Interpretation of Heimito von Doderer's Novel *Ein Mord den jeder begeht.*" *Symposium* 19 (1965): 147 - 54.

SPIEL, HILDE. "Der Kampf gegen das Chaos." *Der Monat* 9:104 (1957): 65 - 68. Reaction to *Die Dämonen.*

STEINER, GEORGE. "The Brown Danube." *Reporter,* October 12, 1961, pp. 58 - 60. Thoroughly venomous reaction to *Die Dämonen.* Vienna is said to be a "provincial town with a somewhat pompous and unsavory past." And the Danube is brown.

STRELKA, JOSEPH P. "Die Tiefe ist aussen, oder Doderers Romantheorie." *Acta Germanica* 5 (1970): 215 - 26.

SWALES, MARTIN W. "The Narrator in the Novels of Heimito von Doderer."

Modern Language Review 61 (1966): 85 - 95. Argues that Doderer's manipulation of the narrator Geyrenhoff of *Die Dämonen* introduces an unnecessarily artificial note. Swales also takes issue with the Kakabsa episodes, which he finds lacking in moral depth.

———. "Ordung und Verworrenheit: Zum Werk Heimito von Doderers." *Wirkendes Wort* 18 (1968): 96 - 130. Order in Doderer's work is interpreted as the largely negative second reality into which we tend to flee. Social reality is *verworren* and has to be accepted as such. In the memory of the past we may perceive unity and order. But this perception is only open to those who have undergone the process of humanization.

TROMMLER, FRANK. "Doderers Moral der Sprache." *Colloquia Germanica* 3 (1971): 283 - 98. Analysis of language as theme. Bringing language into the consciousness of the reader is accomplished by complication and reflection. Stresses Doderer's development and fundamental change in *Der Grenzwald*.

———. "Für eine gerechte Doderer-Fama." *Neues Forum* 15 (1968): 781 - 84. Stresses Doderer's self-inspection and the turn-around exemplified by *Roman No 7*, where even the idea of *Menschwerdung* fades into the background. Cautions against seeing *Die Dämonen* and *Die Strudlhofstiege* as truly representative of Viennese society. Argues that in spite of Doderer's deemphasizing of autobiography, these two novels show his wrestling with aspects of his life.

———. "Naturalist oder Moralist? Zu Doderers Sprache." *Language and Style* 2 (1969): 124 - 31. Critical view of Doderer's stylistic exccrescences and his attempt to combine diagnosis of the ills of his epoch with therapy: raising the level of linguistic consciousness. Condemns Doderer's severe morality, which calls for turning away from social or political action.

TSCHIRKY, RENÉ. *Heimito von Doderers "Posaunen von Jericho": Versuch einer Interpretation*. Philologische Studien und Quellen, 60. Berln: Erich Schmidt, 1971. Detailed survey of the genesis of "Trumpets," which Doderer considered one of his best works. Also detailed explication.

WEBER, DIETRICH. "Heimito von Doderer." In *Deutsche Literatur seit 1945 in Einzeldarstellungen*. Ed. Dietrich Weber. Stuttgart: Kröner, 1968, pp. 77 - 102. One of the pioneers of Doderer criticism writing an authoritative general yet thorough introduction to Doderer.

———. *Heimito von Doderer. Studien zu seinem Romanwerk*. Munich: C. H. Beck, 1963. First monograph on Doderer. Essential reading. Includes thorough bibliography and notes.

WILLIAMS, C. E. "Down a Steep Place. . . : A Study of Heimito von Doderer's *Dämonen*." *Forum for Modern Language Studies* 7:1 (1971): 76 - 82. Argues that Doderer's distinction between political and true history is wrong, and that Doderer's advocacy of individualism is merely a would-be panacea for the ills of European civilization.

Selected Bibliography

WOLFF, LUTZ-WERNER. *Wiedereroberte Aussenwelt: Studien zur Erzählweise Heimito von Doderers am Beispiel des "Romans No 7."* Göppinger Arbeiten zur Germanistik, 13. Göppingen: Kümmerle, 1969. Excellent interpretation of philosophical aspects of Doderer's narratives as well as of individual motifs, as, for example, the *Krebs*.

ZEMAN, HERBERT. "Österreichische Literatur: Zwei Studien." *Jahrbuch der Grillparzer Gesellschaft* 8:3 (1969): 11 - 56. Fascinating investigation of the reflection of late medieval chronicles, which Doderer had studied thoroughly, in his novel *Die Dämonen*. Sees a necessary condition for understanding and *Haltung* in the intertwining of the past and the present.

Index

Absurd, 114
Aristotle, 82

Balzac, Honoré de, 61
Baudelaire, Charles, 25, 26, 54
Beck, C.H. (Biederstein Verlag), 54, 67, 68
Beethoven, Ludwig van, 22, 26, 84
Bildungsroman, 33, 93, 142
Blei, Franz, 21
Broch, Hermann, 92

Camus, Albert, 58

Dauthendey, Max, 26
Divertimento, 27, 28, 53
Doderer, Heimito von

WORKS:
"Begegnung im Morgengrauen," 55-57, 112
Commentarii 1951-1956, 68, 121
Das Geheimnis des Reiches, 19, 36, 52-54, 114, 134, 138
Das letzte Abenteuer, 19, 54, 61-65, 87, 114, 143, 144
"Das russische Land," 23
Der Grenzwald, 19, 124, 125, 133-41
"Der Peinigl," 119
Die Bresche, 25, 28-35, 36, 40, 41, 53, 130
Die Dämonen, 41, 51, 54, 55, 76, 82, 91, 92-110, 122, 133, 135
Die erleuchteten Fenster, 28, 54, 76-79, 81
Die Merowinger, 60, 79, 111, 116-19
"Die Peinigung der Lederbeutelchen," 54, 59-60
"Die Posaunen von Jericho," 111-16
Die Strudlhofstiege, 18, 24, 47, 51, 55, 62, 67, 73, 82, 83-93, 114, 121, 133, 142, 143
Die Wasserfälle von Slunj, 62, 111, 122, 124-33, 134, 135
"Divertimenti I-VI," 41-48
"Ehrfurcht vor dem Alter," 119
Ein Mord den jeder begeht, 54, 68-76
Ein Umweg, 54, 65-67, 87
Ein Weg im Dunklen, 25
"Eine Person von Porzellan," 61
Gassen und Landschaft, 19, 24, 25
"Grundlagen und Funktion des Romans," 35, 84, 85, 86, 111, 121-24
"Jutta Bamberger," 35-41, 53
"Liber Epigrammaticus," 82
"Meine neunzehn Lebensläufe," 20, 34
Repertorium, 83, 120, 121
Roman No VII, 114
Tangenten, 21, 80-82, 121
"Trethofen," 119-20
Wiederkehr der Drachen, 121
"Zwei Lügen oder Eine Antikische Tragödie auf dem Dorfe," 54, 57-59

Dostoyevsky, F.M., 61, 99
Dürrenmatt, Friedrich, 119

Expressionism, 24, 25, 29, 38, 40, 44, 75

Forster, E.M., 84
Freud, Sigmund, 21, 26

Galsworthy, John, 125

Index

George, Stefan, 26
Goethe, Johann Wolfgang von, 64
Grillparzer, Franz, 21
Gütersloh, Albert Paris von, 19, 21, 26, 49-52, 118

Hauptmann, Gerhart, 52
Haybach, Rudolph, 24, 67
Heym, Georg, 38
Homer, 27, 97

Jean Paul, 76, 79
Joyce, James, 35

Kafka, Franz, 26, 79, 119, 143
Kraus, Karl, 20, 21

Lao Tse, 26
Lenau, Nikolaus, 17

Mann, Thomas, 41, 97, 114, 125
Mörike, Eduard, 26
Mozart, Wolfgang Amadeus, 31, 78
Musil, Robert, 35, 92

Naturalism, 50, 51, 61, 84
Nestroy, Johannes, 116

Pirandello, Luigi, 26

Proust, Marcel, 35

"Rashomon," 134
Realism, 61, 107
Rilke, Rainer Maria, 21, 36, 38
roman muet, 122, 125, 139, 141
Romanticism, 82

Schiller, Friedrich, 52
Schopenhauer, Arthur, 23, 26, 27
Spengler, Oswald, 26, 52
Spielhagen, Friedrich, 84
Stifter, Adalbert, 21
Surrealism, 51
Swoboda, Hermann, 21
Symbolism, 25

Thoreau, Henry David, 26
Thomas Aquinas, 35, 124
totaler Roman, 50, 51

Unamuno, 26, 27

Valéry, Paul, 25

Wagner, Richard, 26
Weininger, Otto, 21
Wilde, Oscar, 26

Zola, Émile, 26